Gum-Dipped

A Daughter Remembers
Rubber Town

☙☙☙

Gum-Dipped

A Daughter Remembers
Rubber Town

Joyce Dyer

The University of Akron Press
Akron, Ohio

Library of Congress has cataloged the hardcover edition of this book as follows.
Dyer, Joyce.
    Gum-dipped : a daughter remembers Rubber Town /
Joyce A. Dyer.
       p. cm. — (Series on Ohio history and culture)
    ISBN 1-884836-99-2 (alk. paper)
      1. Akron (Ohio)—History.   2. Akron (Ohio)—Biography.
3. Coyne, Tom, 1911–1990.   4. Dyer, Joyce.   5. Firestone Tire
and Rubber Company.   6. Fathers and daughters.   I. Title.
II. Series.
F499.A3 D94 2003
977.1'36043'092—dc21
                                        2003008850
        ISBN 1-931968-17-9 (pbk.: alk. paper)

To Daniel

To break so vast a Heart

Required a Blow as vast—

No Zephyr felled this Cedar straight—

'Twas undeserved Blast—

—Emily Dickinson

☙☙☙

CONTENTS

❦❦

Contents

PREFACE

I sometimes wish I didn't need the smell of rubber, but I do.

Its smell ignites my memory. My father returns to me in that odor. When tires spin too fast on hot roads, I think of Tom Coyne, or when I smell steam on the flat rubber roof of our house after a summer rain.

When no one's looking, I run my hands over the tubes that feed gasoline into my car, over the handles of the Airdyne that I ride, over mousepads and the backs of rugs. I snap rows of rubber bands onto my arms, like bracelets, until they cut my wrists.

Over and over I dream of tires—huge tires with treads the shape of diamonds, or arrowheads—rolling fast down highways. Chasing me. I always wake up before I know if I escape.

In Akron rubber workers were known as *gummers,* and managers were sometimes said to be *gum-dipped.* The term came from the process of dipping strips of cloth in rubber until they were completely coated and uniform, and then adding the strips to tread for greater strength and flexibility. In the early years Firestone Gum-Dipped tires were the deluxe line—the very best.

This is one story of rubber, of both a gummer and a gum-dipped man, of a daughter who was as immersed in rubber as he was, of a family who thought for a long time that they were riding on the very best.

I have tried to be meticulous about my research not only because

I write nonfiction, but because I so strongly believe that if we understand the ordinary and the real, and marvel at *it*, we will see far more
than we ever could if we made things up. I apologize for any errors
Akron historians may find in these pages, because none were intended.

But the interpretation and speculation here are *mine*, and the
scenes I include are the product of *my* memory only. I urge you to remember this as you read about Firestone Park and the rubber industry in the middle decades of the last century. What is important to
one person may go unnoticed by another. My elaboration of some
details over others is consistent with the effect they had on me, but I
can't argue that others should have found them as memorable as I
did.

It's history that you will read here, but sometimes very personal
and impressionistic history. It's the story of Akron, of Firestone
Park, of the Firestone Tire & Rubber Company, of my family, but always as it appears to me, and to *no one else*. I cannot help the curva-
ture of my own eye. I've tried to see as much as I'm able at this point
in my life, but I know I may have missed something that later will
come clear to me.

ACKNOWLEDGMENTS

I've been educated by the people of Akron, Ohio, all my life. Certainly this book is no exception. Much of my research was interior, but much of it was not. Eudora Welty talks about the relationship of memory and discovery in her memoir, *One Writer's Beginnings.* "As we discover, we remember; remembering, we discover," she writes. I want to thank many people for helping me make discoveries that in turn fired my memory, and then led to other discoveries I could never have anticipated. I must begin by thanking the excellent staff at the University of Akron Archives in the Polsky Building—John Miller, Stephen Paschen, Craig Holbert, and George Hodowanec. Meticulous and resourceful scholars of the region, they were always patient with my unending questions through the many months I worked with them.

Through them I met Jim Paulau, Akron's premier architectural historian; Sylvia Johnson, lifelong resident of Firestone Park and Director of Hower House; Earlene Harris, who introduced me to books by Firestone Park aficionados Lois Finley and Clarice Finley Lewis; Sarah and Stan Akers, true preservationists of Akron history; William Lewis, Director of the Buckingham Lyle Center; Daniel Nelson, labor historian at the University of Akron; and Claudia Burdge, Head of the City of Akron Department of Planning Library.

I would also like to thank many others for vital information about Akron or Summit County. They include Lyle Skinner, Coordinator with the United Steelworkers of America, and Donald Tucker, URW District One Director in the 1970s. Ben Kastein, a former Firestone chemist, helped me understand the processes of vulcanizing and reclaiming rubber. Others who also took time to speak with me include William Hahn, Akron City Arborist and Horticulturalist; Bill Spaulding, Superintendent of Parks for Akron, who grew up just a few streets from my house; Gene Rohrbough, Principal of Firestone Park Elementary School and a former high-school classmate (with special thanks to the PTA for preserving wonderful scrapbooks from the 1950s); Jerry Taylor, Akron Board of Education School Architect; Thomas Luck, owner of Lucky's Shoes in Fairlawn; the late James Caccamo, Hudson Library and Historical Society Archivist until his untimely death. I am grateful, as well, to employees and friends of Bridgestone/Firestone who helped me with the history of the company.

I would especially like to thank members of my family who supported me throughout the writing of this book. They helped me bring things into sharper focus and sometimes told me stories I had not known. These wonderful people include Carol Zink, Tonya Santos, Wendell Scott, Marjorie Davis, Ralph E. Kane, Paul Steurer Jr., and Paul Steurer Sr.—who was known as the Heart of Goosetown to everyone on Grant Street, the street where he was born and recently died. I would also like to thank Audrey Calhoun, a relative on my husband's side who talked to me about polio, and Prudence Dyer, Richard Dyer, Davis Dyer, Janice McCormick, Bella McCormick Dyer, and Ricky McCormick Dyer for their tireless encouragement.

Although many Akron employees must go unnamed here, I want them to know I appreciate their help locating information. They work in the Akron Courthouse, the Harold K. Stubbs Justice Center, the Municipal Building, the Morley Health Center, the Ocasek Building, the Ohio Building, Bridgestone/Firestone, Akron churches and cemeteries, Akron bookstores, the Akron-Summit County Public Library, Akron law offices, Bierce Library, the Kent State University Library and Special Collections, the Akron Public Schools, and Akron museums.

I would also like to thank the librarians at Hiram College for helping me lay the groundwork for this book; Candy Painley, Missie Mallinak, and Chris Niemi for their technical assistance; and Hiram College itself for generously granting me a sabbatical to begin the research for this book. Funding from the Michael Dively Summer Scholar Award and the Michael Dively Endowment for Scholarly Publications was especially important to the completion of my manuscript.

The University of Akron Press, especially Director Michael J. Carley, Production Coordinator Amy Petersen, and Marketing Representatives Jodi Arment and Julie Roberts, generously and creatively advised me throughout the production process.

I extend great thanks to *Akron Beacon Journal* staff writers who have done a thorough and passionate job of documenting Akron's history since 1839. Due to their efforts, as well as the efforts of WPA workers who indexed *Beacon* issues from 1841 to 1939, the history of my own Akron family has been preserved and made available to me. Steve Love and David Giffels, authors of *Wheels of Fortune: The Story of Rubber in Akron,* deserve special mention for their careful documentation of the history of rubber in Akron, Ohio, and for their passion for this subject.

I want to thank another *Akron Beacon Journal* staff writer, Stephen Osborn Dyer, my son, for his enthusiasm for Akron and family history, and his excellent editorial sense. I also greatly appreciated the encouragement of Stephen's wife, Melissa McGowan Dyer.

Finally, I thank my husband, Daniel Osborn Dyer, for so generously sharing with me his ear for language and his loving heart.

It Was Moving Day . . .

Harvey Firestone looked a lot like Lincoln sitting there. That's what I thought when I was young, anyway. It didn't matter to me that Harvey's statue was bronze, not marble, or that he sat on a hill in south Akron rather than on the banks of the Potomac.

In my young eyes, the two men looked nearly the same. Harvey and Abe. Abe and Harvey.

I was staring at Harvey again, this time from a folding chair. It was August 3, 2000, the Centennial of the Firestone Tire & Rubber Company, and the fiftieth anniversary of the original Dedication of the Firestone statue. I had written a letter begging the Firestone Centennial Committee to invite me to the ceremony.

I told them that I belonged as much as anyone else on that twenty-five-acre hill in south Akron where Harvey sat. The hill marked the entrance to Firestone Park, the community Akron's rubber baron began building for his workers in 1916—and the place where I grew up decades later.

I explained that my mother's cousins and uncles had been blacksmiths and roofers, lab technicians and photographers at Firestone. Her father, August Haberkost, had worked for Firestone shortly after the company was founded in Akron on August 3, 1900 (the entire factory force numbered twenty-seven in 1903). My paternal grandfather, W. T. (William Thomas) Coyne, had traveled in 1923 from the anthracite coal mines in Pennsylvania to help Harvey keep his books and had retired thirty years later as comptroller of a Firestone subsidiary plant. T. W. (Thomas William) Coyne, my father, was a thirty-seven-year man who had spent most of his life as a supervisor at the Xylos Rubber Company, Firestone's reclaim plant.

In many ways, I said, the history of the company and the history of my family were identical. The Coynes and Haberkosts who had spent their lives building Firestone tires were all dead now, so I just had to be on that high summit overlooking Harvey's empire to represent them.

The committee agreed and sent me a formal invitation, just like the ones executives received.

I spent that August night with people who talked only about Firestone, and it was all I talked about too. I never suspected that the company at that moment was coming unhinged, that in the next few days Bridgestone/Firestone would begin recalling 6.5 million tires, most of them on Ford Explorers, or that the federal government would soon link faulty Firestone tires to 203 deaths and more than 700 injuries. In May 2001, the Ford Motor Company would announce another recall and replace an additional 13 million Firestone Wilderness AT tires on its vehicles—at a cost of 3 billion dollars—a decision that would cause Firestone to sever a nearly century-old corporate and personal relationship with the world's second-largest automaker. Firestone would no longer sell tires to Ford, even though Ford's chairman, William Clay Ford Jr., was the grandson of Harvey S. Firestone Jr., and the unity of the two families had been solidly demonstrated when the Firestone homestead was dismantled in 1985 and moved to the Henry Ford Museum & Greenfield Village in Dearborn, Michigan.

The National Highway Traffic Safety Administration would investigate Firestone and find it at fault. The wedge, the section of rubber where the tread meets the shoulder, had not been thick enough—a deadly design flaw. Firestone would be forced to call back 3.5 million more tires.

I suspected nothing about the imminent crisis that night, though since my father's death ten years before I'd found out secrets that should have led me to suspect. For decades my father had been blind too, refusing to see what Firestone would do to him one day.

There I sat, his daughter, staring at the truth, but not able to see it.

I guess a part of me still wanted to believe in Harvey the way I used to, wanted to turn the clock back and become, once more, the daughter of a man who so long ago had signed over his heart, and then his soul, to the company he loved.

For years and years that faith sustained him.

It sustained me too. When I was young, every time I saw the statue or touched a tire, every time I swung on Harvey's swings in Harvey's park or watched a circus the great man brought to entertain us, I pledged my allegiance to Harvey S. Firestone. I thanked God—who looked an awful lot like Harvey in my mind—for the Firestone Tire & Rubber Company.

The Firestone Tire & Rubber Company factory complex

CHAPTER 1

My dad reached out the window of our Hudson Hornet and tapped the ash from his Camel. His finger struck the paper fast, as if it were made of pure nerve, not bone.

We were driving down Main Street in the fall of 1952. It was moving day and I was five years old and we had just bought a little Tudor house in Firestone Park with ivy and purple clematis that crept up the sides.

The Tom Coynes would never move again. I would leave, but they would stay and finish out their lives there.

To get to Firestone Park from our old neighborhood of Goosetown, my father could have driven south on Grant Street or Brown, but he took Main Street instead—Harvey's road, the road that ran parallel to the factories. In my father's mind, South Main was the road to everything he cared about, and he wasn't going to drive down any other.

We drove past the Firestone Bank. That was *always* our bank, and now it held our new mortgage. After we crossed the Harvey S. Firestone Memorial Bridge and approached the mile-long factory complex, my dad began to ask me to name the buildings as they came into view, just the way he did on less momentous trips.

"Clubhouse!" I screamed, as our car wobbled over railroad tracks.

My father smiled, then snapped his head toward the building

and away from the road, a habit that always made my mother nervous. I thought it was funny—it made my dad look like a cartoon—and I usually laughed.

Then my father told me to look up.

"Look at *that!*" he said, pointing with his right arm, his white sleeves rolled to the elbow, the way they always were when he wasn't working at the plant. I saw the huge red neon Firestone sign glowing on the flat roof of Plant 1.

We slowed down when we came to Emerling Street, between those two main plants. It was a sacred road to my dad. Every morning he would climb in his car, drive down Main Street, and turn onto Emerling—the street that dead-ended right at the Xylos Rubber Company, where my father worked. He would wait for the attendant at the gatehouse to nod and say, "Mornin', Mr. Coyne!" and then greet the guard, smile widely, wheel his car into the parking space reserved *just* for him—because he was a foreman now and had a piece of pavement all his own.

Beyond Emerling was Plant 2 and the Firestone Stadium. And on the east side of Main Street, right across the street from all of this, was Harvey's hill—the hill that marked the entrance to Firestone Park. My father turned onto Firestone Boulevard and stopped the car.

He'd spotted Harvey first.

Dedicated in 1950, the statue of Harvey Firestone was just two years old when we arrived. A huge field of green dotted with wildflowers spread from the corner all the way to the bronze figure that was gleaming in morning light at the top of the knob.

"Mmm, mmm!" my father said, smacking his lips the same way he did when he ate a steak.

Seated on a huge throne, Harvey seemed to be watching each car as it turned into his kingdom.

Xylos Rubber Company, 1934 (Courtesy of Bridgestone/Firestone, Inc.)

I had seen it before, but somehow that day it was larger and brighter than I'd remembered it. How could I resist a thing like that statue when I was five years old? There was nothing like it in all of Goosetown, where swings and slides, a merry-go-round and teeter-totters were all we had to play on in Thornton Park.

There were statues downtown that I had seen before I saw Harvey, but none of them amazed me the way Harvey did. There were two stone lions at the foot of the courthouse stairs, and two other stone figures (one with a sword and one sort of thinking) near the doors. In the park by the courthouse was a bronze of Charles

Goodyear in a bow tie and a coat with tails. In front of the Akron Armory stood a pretty exciting metal statue of a WWI soldier in full uniform, grenade in one hand and rifle in the other. And of course in Washington, D.C., there was Lincoln, Harvey's statue look-alike, but we saw him only on vacations.

To me Harvey Firestone was better than a lion or a soldier or even Lincoln himself. He was a *king* up there on the top of his hill, in the midst of meadow and forest with birds singing everywhere. It was Harvey who reigned where I was moving, who built our Tudor house, who cut our curved streets and bought fancy little streetlights that glowed into our bedroom windows, who loved my father, and therefore must love me. Harvey was mine.

We'd just studied heaven in Sunday school the summer before our move, and I thought about it all the time. I was sure this was heaven we were driving toward that autumn day, sure that Firestone Park would have golden streets and children in glory robes biking in the air. All the bikes would be golden, even the spokes, and kids would peel across the sky ringing golden bells set on golden handlebars and singing the Firestone jingle like angels, singing it more joyfully than even Harvey's singers on the radio, or my own father sang it in the shower before he dressed for work, or I did when I skipped to school. The words would just fly from their lips, as natural as breath. "Wherever wheels are rolling" (the voices would begin), "No matter what the load" (the bike angels would trill, wings fluttering and halos spinning as their voices rose to true angel height), "The name that's known is Firestone, Where the rubber meets the road!"

Tires seldom met the road in my fantasy, I admit, spinning like that in the air on bikes driven by angels. But they were still always *tires*—black things with tread—true to the spirit of the jingle. Even in

Harvey S. Firestone statue (Photograph by Russ Vitale, 2000.
Courtesy of Bridgestone/Firestone, Inc.)

a fantasy as colorful as mine, I never turned the tires to gold, *never,* because even then I knew that rubber was greater than gold, and there was no way heaven could improve on it. Rubber had brought us here. We were made of water and bones and minerals, like other people, but we were made of rubber too. Latex flowed through our veins and kept us alive.

Fifty years before our move, Harvey Sr. lifted his small son in the air and let him throw the switch that sent into motion a mill, a washer, and two boilers in an abandoned building on Sweitzer and Miller Avenues. His first factory. At that same moment, Harvey's unborn workers—in Akron, West Virginia, or Pennsylvania, like my dad—felt the current that would one day bring them all to life.

CHAPTER 2

❧❧

My father's dreams were a little more practical than mine. Tom Coyne wanted to own a house in Firestone Park—a house with 1359 square feet and a monthly mortgage of $61. I think he may have dreamed about that house for the first time the day he came home from World War II and pulled into his Goosetown drive.

He didn't stay until the war was over, like other soldiers. It wasn't that he'd worn his welcome out, or done anything wrong. The army liked my dad well enough.

It was just that Firestone liked him *more.* At least in the 1940s.

The War Department had released him into the care of the Firestone Tire & Rubber Company so he could be a Soldier of Production and build truck tires for vehicles that would carry the Allies to victory. Tom Coyne was needed back home.

My dad was an army MP. He was a *guard* by nature, a man who liked safety—not a warrior. When he returned to Xylos, he transferred to the Enlisted Reserve Corp (ERC) and became an air raid warden—serving as a guard even on the home front. The last thing Tom Coyne would have wanted was to pull a trigger. As far as I know, he never fired a single bullet from the .45 the army strapped to his right side, and was probably relieved to find out he had to turn in his gun when they handed him his discharge papers.

He stored a few relics from the war in our attic, but they were all items that *protected* a soldier, not ones that helped him kill. He

Annabelle and T. W. Coyne

brought home a foldup shovel that hangs in my garage now and I use in the fall to plant tulip bulbs, a helmet and a gas mask that my son keeps somewhere in the attic of his condo, and a painting of Fort Leonard Wood that a man made for my dad. There were no knives, no unexploded hand grenades, no bayonets, no macabre souvenirs— fingers, hair, guns—from dead enemies. On Veterans Day each year I'd hear my father pull down the chain to the disappearing attic stairs in the upstairs hall, and head to his collection for his annual inspection. I don't know what he did there, exactly, but when he returned he sat in the living room and talked non-stop about jeeps and trucks, officers he liked, and the Thanksgiving menu at the fort. He talked faster than normal for about half an hour—unaware that I was sitting next to him—and then just stopped. He'd spot his razor on the windowsill, turn it on, and begin to shave.

Danger was something my dad *always* worked hard to avoid, and I think when he returned to our old neighborhood of Goosetown its hazards became more visible to him, and his dream of a house in Firestone Park became more real.

Goosetown may have looked too much like the war to my father, may have seemed unmanageable to Tom Coyne the day my mother met him at the Union Depot and handed him the keys to their 1940 Dodge sedan. The fear he had to hide just under his skin all those long months away from home may have crawled right out of him and taken the shape of the shadows he saw in Goosetown's alleyways.

But shades had always haunted Goosetown, long before my father found them there.

Goosetown had been settled in the nineteenth century by German immigrants, the largest ethnic population in greater Akron in its early years, and the largest still. It was a place as hard as the ledges that formed it. Below the surface were limestone, shale, sandstone.

Wolf Run eroded a ravine in Goosetown and gave it its second name: Old Wolf Ledge. My maternal grandparents, August Haberkost and Anna Golz, grew up climbing the rock ledges of Old Wolf Run, and I imagine them trading their first hard kiss with their backs pressed against the rocks—a hole right in front of them as big as a crater on the moon. They were lucky they didn't die on that terrain, because people did.

Goosetown wasn't, of course, as hard a place when my mother grew up there on Grant Street in the 1910s and 1920s, when my father lived there on Gray Avenue after coming from Pennsylvania in 1923, or when my mother and father lived there together on Eagle Street after they were married in 1936. It was never an *easy* place, but I don't think it was as dangerous during those years as it was when my maternal grandparents roamed Wolf Ledges in the nineteenth century. In 1894 Sumner Street was graded and the gorge was filled in and the Sumner Street Bridge was buried. But before that there wasn't even a guardrail for protection, and once a baby buggy went over the cliff into the creek bed and a child died. The child's father, Fritz Koerschner, collected money from the city for damages and with it started a saloon at the corner of Grant and South.

That was one of the many saloons frequented by my grandfather. I think it was August Haberkost, and the kind of man he was, that rose up in my father's mind when he thought about returning to Goosetown. Every night before he left, and every night after he returned, my father and my uncles would listen out their windows for the violent voice and sounds of this man who put them always on alert. They would take a little bag with a comb and a toothbrush and sit in August's house—*his* guards—until the old man sobered up and decided to behave himself. They would often stay all night, grabbing August's arms when they whirled toward his wife.

Burger Brewing Company of Cincinnati bought Burkhardt Brewery in 1957, so most people don't remember the name Burkhardt anymore. But I do. It's true I don't remember the original brew house that my grandparents knew in the 1880s, because it was replaced with a six-story building after the turn of the century, but the new buildings and the old were essentially on the same spot and sent about the same odor into *our* air as the air my grandpa breathed in the nineteenth century.

My grandpa's house was only one block from the brewery, and the house and the brewery smelled the same to me when I lived in Goosetown. Grandpa always, *always* had a bottle of beer in his hand, and another by his rocking chair. When I see the German Tyrol with a bristle in his hat and a mustache and giant nose, I think of August Haberkost, and I never smile.

It was all connected. The saloons, the brewery, my grandfather's terrible addiction. Water for Burkhardt beer was taken from Wolf Creek, the same creek my grandpa walked when he was young. His baptismal creek. Every day he walked that creek, until he finally arrived, all grown up, at the doors of the brewery.

In 1964 all brewing stopped on Grant Street. Eventually the bottling plant was purchased by the Akron Public Schools for offices. The brew house is still there, but it's broken everywhere. When I look at those buildings, though, they seem the same as they were almost fifty years ago. They *always* looked angry to me, just as angry as I remember Anna being when she stared across at them from her Grant Street house. Now I wonder if those buildings may have looked angry to my father too when he came home from war, even though he knew a part of him loved the brewery just the way my grandpa did. Maybe that's one reason he wanted out. Maybe he chose to run from that thing inside of him that he had watched destroy my mother's dad, my mother's home.

August had explored all the treasures in that brewery, the way he had explored the creek that led to it when he was young. It held all the mystery he ever knew. He loved the colors of beers, the caramel taste they had, the glass bottles that were the only decorations in his life. But Anna's own mysteries went unnoticed by him. Perhaps my dad knew that if he didn't leave, his *own* Anna—my mother, Annabelle—might be forgotten too. Perhaps at that moment he chose the mystery of my mother's hair (it was as blond the day she died as the day she was born, just as her own mother's brown hair never changed), her athleticism, her pure blue eyes, her quick mind, her transparent heart—instead of the mystery of that golden liquid that had mesmerized so many Goosetown men.

I wonder, too, if my dad felt nervous coming home to a place as German as Goosetown was. There were German clubs and societies everywhere. Neighbors still spoke German in their backyards and over counters of corner grocery stores. The Akron Turner Club and Turner Hall, the Sons of Herman, the German American Mutual Aid Society were all just a block or two away from my parents' home on Eagle Street. The Turner Club was where my mother learned to dance.

My Irish father had lived on a Goosetown street his teenage years, had fallen in love with a German woman, and as a married man had ended up renting a house from a German family just a block away from August Haberkost—who still goosesteps down Grant Street in my dreams. But my father *wasn't* German, and he had gone away to learn how to hate Germans. Goosetown must have been a confusing place for him when he returned. Old loves stood beside new suspicions, and former hatreds may have found a form. Did Tom Coyne see the Führer now when he held the straight arm of August from his wife's soft skin?

Even Goosetown's houses may have looked meaner than they

did before to the thin soldier behind the wheel of that Dodge. August and Anna had a house with a small front porch and gray asphalt siding. It always looked old—but not in the handsome way our English Tudor looked old. The Tudor looked like history, like a castle in a book, like Shakespeare's house, but the Grant Street house just looked old, like Grandma, and sagged everywhere just the way that she did. The sound of the player piano Anna and August got from Lord-knows-where and kept against a wall in their living room was the only joyful noise I ever heard inside.

The house *we* lived in on Eagle Street may have reminded Tom Coyne of his barracks. It had been quickly built and not intended to last much beyond Akron's first rubber boom. Literally raised in someone's backyard, it was a cheap, skinny house—as skinny as my dad was back then—with a furnace that took more vacations than we did and tall wire fences between all the backyards. I imagine my dad glancing through the panes of his windshield, noticing for the first time how close the houses really were, and hating the way that sunlight exploded into his eyes off fences that rose like metal vines.

I think Tom Coyne saw danger everywhere. He may have leaned over to my mother in the car that day, with his discharge papers flowering from his pockets like a huge white peony, and promised her something better than this. He may have brought her a small gift, perhaps a rhinestone pin in a pearl box, and placed it in her hands with the soft promise of quiet streets and easy soil that she could turn with a trowel, like the flesh of fish.

༂ལྑཛ

A house in the Park was not something my parents could afford in 1944 when Dad returned from the war that was not yet over, or even three years later, after I was born. But from the time that I was old enough to realize my parents were separate from me, I knew this

T. W. Coyne fishing at Aunt Lil's lake in Portage Lakes

was their dream, and thought of it whenever I thought of them. There was Tom and Annabelle and the House that they would find together, the three things soldered in my mind. My parents were always talking about saving money and *down payments,* and writing on the ledger sheets of tiny blue and maroon bankbooks. I remember them sitting in the living room hunched over rows and rows of numbers on small-lined paper.

But it was our trips to Portage Lakes to visit Aunt Lil and Uncle Mike that sent the strongest signal to me about my parents' wish to leave the only place my mother had ever lived. On weekends we would pack the car and visit our *lake* relatives. My father didn't even like water, but he liked the idea of a house on the lake, the idea of houses with great backyards wet with worms, with fruit trees that divided lots instead of wire fences, with water in the background, not angry cars. He sometimes fished, but always kept his feet on the shoreline.

Portage Lakes were just south of Goosetown, and it took us less than ten minutes to get there. It was a world made entirely of water, completely different from the world of metal and hard earth on Eagle Street. Traveling there always felt like a vacation: My father talked about our visits to the lakes with the same excitement I heard in his voice when he planned our trips to Florida at the height of summer—the off-season when the rates were low and the temperatures were in the 100s, when no one in their right mind would be booking rooms at the Hollywood Beach Hotel except the Tom Coynes of Akron, Ohio, *because we'd have the place all to ourselves, honey, and it's cheap!*

I closed my eyes in the back seat and held my breath. If I stopped my ears and did this noisy thing with my tongue clicking on the roof of my mouth, the trip always seemed to take a little longer than it really did. The only way I knew to make time slow down was to stop sensation from striking me, to find a way to keep my heart from beating as fast and hard as it often did.

My two favorite cousins sometimes went along. Paul, Aunt Ruth and Uncle Paul's son, and Carol, Aunt Marie's daughter. I was an only child and my parents always said they were *so sorry* and invited my cousins everywhere, as if I had an illness or something and would die if I were left alone.

The three of us had learned about the Delaware Indians in school and sort of knew they once lived here, near the Cuyahoga and Tuscarawas Rivers, so we'd pretend we were Indians too, camping on the shores of Aunt Lil's lake. As Uncle Mike steered us in his motorboat, I'd imagine I was an Indian princess in a canoe, though the image in my mind, I'm afraid, was of myself in the Indian costume I wore for a Jean Shepherd dance recital at Loew's Theater, a cream thing with a sequined halter and short pants decorated with silky fringe, and a bright red plume supported by a headband studded with colored rhinestones. It was a bizarre costume to begin with—what real Indian would *ever* dress like that in the forests of Ohio?—but especially bizarre on the stage of a theater like Loew's whose interior was designed to resemble a Moorish palace, complete with twinkling stars and drifting clouds on the ceiling. *I* thought the whole thing was spectacular.

We searched for arrowheads in the mud by the water, then fastened them to sticks with ground ivy and string, or the rubber bands kids from Rubber Town always carried in their pockets.

Back then I was sure that all of history occurred in three days. I didn't even have the patience to wait for the world to be created in *six,* the way the Bible said it was.

A girl from one of Akron's fundamentalist Baptist churches be-

*Paul Steurer Jr. and author in Indian costumes for a
Jean Shepherd dance recital*

gan cornering me in the coatroom of our elementary school shortly
after we moved to the Park, hoping to convince me to believe in
Genesis. She was worried that I liked dinosaurs because I always
stared at them in picture books in the library. She had picked me out
as someone who might believe in *that godless evolution.* Someone
who might need help.

She talked about dinosaurs all the time, saying how stupid it was
to think they ever really lived. Her father was a minister and sometimes she would ask me to sleep over on Saturday nights so that she

could tell me about creation and God in bed and then take me to church on Sunday morning. I always went because she had nice skin, these two weird dog teeth that poked into her lower lip, and hair as thick as fur cut in a Buster Brown style I really liked.

She wasted a lot of missionary zeal on me. The idea of evolution would have been impossible for me to have embraced back then—even a *six-day* theory was stretching it. On my timeline there was only *today, yesterday* (if I really worked hard to remember it), and *tomorrow.* That was it. Summer days were divided into morning, afternoon, and evening, but they were all the same, and they were all accomplished on a bike moving straight through time.

In the morning I fed my parakeet and handed clothespins to my aunt, who took care of me while my mother worked. We raced down the lines before the sun was up, trying to give the sheets time to dry before soot from Firestone swept up the hill and into our backyard. At noon the Hymn for the Day played on Firestone radios all over the Park as we ate Campbell's alphabet soup. When we saw those pasta letters that floated on the broth, we knew the afternoon had begun. We mounted our bikes for the sixteen-acre park at the center of our community after we'd coaxed the last *s* or *d* from the side of our bowls onto our spoons. At five o'clock we returned to suppers of meat loaf and mashed potatoes in the little breakfast nooks Firestone Park was famous for, and then waited for a second nod that sent us rushing to homes on the Boulevard of friends with big backyards and badminton nets or croquet sets.

I guess I should tell now about the evening fights my parents had, and their affairs, and the terrible anger of my very smart mother, who married a man who was probably not nearly her equal on the IQ charts and bored her to death. But these things simply did not exist in my home. My parents had both lived hard lives—my mother the daughter of a fierce drunk, and one of seven children. By ten she had strapped on the apron she would not remove for seven years, working in a local grocery store, selling striped boxes of Kirkman's potato chips and Oh Henry! bars from glass bowls to make money because her daddy had forgotten how. Maybe she *never* removed that apron again, as I think about it now.

My father made mistakes when he was young, but knew my mother wasn't one of them. Before they married he wrote love letters to her that I store in the bottom of my jewelry box and read when I lose faith in the world. Every day that he looked across our little breakfast table into my mother's face, I could feel the thing that joined them, as real as the safety bar you pull down on the seat of a carnival ride. I never remember him noticing anything about her—a new blouse, a permanent, a bright pin she may have bought at a five-and-dime—except that she was *there,* or that she wasn't.

They had learned their love in the Depression, and they somehow always knew how lucky they were to have it, this strong thing between them that wasn't sex or romance and had no place for jealousy. They were always very silent with each other, almost as if they were listening for the next hard thing their love would need to get them through.

And there would be many of those to come, betrayals much larger than something as small and ordinary as the roving eye of a man.

My days were predictable then, as predictable as my parents' love. For a long time I confused the two. My parents were always there, and the day was always there, and their routines and mine were the slow, steady beats that called me everywhere. When I went to the lake, though, I left the world my parents had made for me, and in a way, I left them *too.* The world and time gained dimension at Aunt Lil's lake.

The clock was just as regular on the lake. It wasn't that. There were motorboats and picnic tables, and there was always Aunt Lil standing in the yard with her arms folded over her great belly. There were the rituals—the best times to fish and boat, and always a simple lunch. But you might find an arrowhead nudging up through the ground when you least expected to. Time was dense and thick on the lake. It didn't just move straight ahead, the way it did at home. It was not just an arrow sailing forward in front of me. At Aunt Lil's it arced, fell, then pierced the ground and burrowed in. Stories were old and edged beneath my feet, waiting for me to find them.

☙❧

We went to the lake for many years, though more often—and always more eagerly—when we lived on Eagle Street. I remember the sadness in our car when it was time to go back home. Back to houses boxed in by other homes, to poor furnaces, noisy pipes, broken windows, and—*always*—to the two boys who lived next door.

The rubber companies had intended that housing constructed during the first rubber boom between 1910 and 1920 be temporary—including the house we rented on Eagle Street. But people like us were eager to live in something inexpensive, so no one talked very hard about tearing any buildings down. Some people *had* to live in something cheap, my dad was fond of saying, but the Tom Coynes *chose* to live in Goosetown so they could save for a house in the Park.

Wire mesh fences were just a fact of Goosetown life. They rose up and stretched everywhere. There was a fenced-in pen for our dog and on three sides of the small lot that we rented a five-foot fence for me. I learned to stand by grabbing those wires, pulling myself up, sometimes scoring my palms.

For the first five years of my life, I looked at the world through the rectangles of that fence. The wires broke things up and organized everything I saw in front of me. I would frame objects between

*Author holding onto fence in backyard of Eagle Street
house in Goosetown*

the metal lines, like pages in a book. Through one, I might see a
cloud and a piece of a neighbor's clothesline. Through another,
buckeyes shining on the ground at me like dark bright eyes the earth
had grown.

The fence kept balls and bats and toys off our property, and, for a
while, it kept the boys who owned them on the other side. I still
knew the boys were there, of course, but felt about them the way I
might about a mean dog behind a gate. I knew they were mean, and

jumped a little when I heard something that resembled a human growl or bark coming from their side, but I didn't really think they'd ever get in, or they'd ever get *me*. They sometimes sprayed me with a garden hose through the holes when they were filling their rubber swimming pool, or said things that sounded ugly and made me move to the other side of our yard. *I'm gonna throw dog poo on you! Think I'll pee in your ugly little face!* But I got used to them, the way you get used to anything that frightens you but does no harm, like a scary record playing in another room, whose fiercest bands you come to know and just press out with your fingertips against your ears.

Before long, though, the boys discovered they could enter the backyard through a little gate at the *front* of our property. There was no way to stop them once they figured *that* out. One day, when they knew my parents were inside, and our dog was locked in his pen, they decided to come over and toss around the tops of tin cans. They didn't ask me if I wanted to play, but just began sailing lids in my direction. It looked like fun, so I lifted my arms and began to pinch the air with both hands.

We may have invented the Frisbee that day.

My first successful catch was so exciting that I started doing this stupid little jump and couldn't stop. I must have had my eyes closed, or maybe just was moving so fast vertically that for a minute I lost all connection to the horizontal world, forgetting it was even there. A second lid flew toward me and I found myself sitting on the ground with a piece of tin stuck in my forehead.

Blood spilled down my cheeks and dripped from my chin. All I could do was howl. It scared the boys away, and brought my parents outside.

They pulled out the lid and my father pressed his handkerchief over the wound, gently, but as hard as I could stand. He scooped me up while my mother wrapped my head in a towel, and together they

*Cousins Carol King, author, and Paul Steurer Jr. swinging in
Thornton Park, Goosetown*

carried me to our car and we zoomed across town to the emergency
room. It was as if they knew exactly what to do and they did it in one
continuous motion. By the time it was over, I didn't know where the
injury had stopped and the treatment begun. The pain from the
shots and ten stitches seemed every bit as bad—maybe even worse—
than a tin Frisbee in my skull.

✍✍

During the early 1950s there were other things happening in
Goosetown that my father might not have liked besides errant lids of
cans. Things that fed his dream of moving to the Park. People were

beginning to find broken glass on the bottom of the swimming pool in Thornton Park, and Grant Street—Goosetown's main thoroughfare—had recently been resurfaced, causing traffic to pick up a little. You could sometimes hear brakes squealing now, and at night more horns and sirens than we'd ever heard before. In the summertime my father turned his Firestone radio way up to let the *CBS Radio Mystery Theater* he always listened to in bed drown out the cars. The radio was so loud that for a while I thought the people in the play lived in the wall between my parents' room and mine. An automatic timer choked the sound exactly half an hour after I heard my dad's first snore, strangling the people who lived insides the walls.

Rent was rising—from fifteen dollars, when my father left for war, to thirty-five, then forty. And nothing got better for the extra money. Cold seeped through every seam of that house during brutal Ohio winters, and then it seeped through us. The house had outlived its life, the landlord said, and there was nothing he could do.

It took just one more thing to send us racing from Goosetown.

Eddie had to die.

My five-year-old cousin had been sent by our grandmother to get a Popsicle at the Davis Service Store on Grant Street, just north of Grandma's house. He held the hand of his six-year-old sister, Carol, just as he was instructed to. He'd done this *many* times, and always come home. Carol was one of my two special cousins who traveled with me to Aunt Lil's house. I guess Eddie would have been the third, if he had lived.

Grandma made the mistake of trusting the streets of Goosetown. I don't know why, really, but she did. I think I'd have to study Goosetown a long, long time in order to find anything that resembles an answer to that hard question. I know that when Anna

Haberkost was ten years old, in 1890, a tornado had ripped through Akron. It destroyed wooden sheds and an icehouse at the Burkhardt Brewing Company. She must have heard it roaring toward Grant and Goosetown, then heard it veer north, toward the brewery and downtown, instead of south, toward her house. Maybe she heard her mother say it was luck that it had turned that way. A good omen. It had ruined other people's lives, but not theirs. Maybe she thought that kind of trouble on the outside would always whirl away from her, because there had been so many other kinds that took up space *inside* the Grant Street house after she married August in 1904.

For reasons I may never know, Grandma let the children go alone.

The afternoon Eddie died was unusually hot. Ninety-five degrees. Akron hadn't known heat like that in twenty years. Eddie was just a small boy and had *never* felt such heat before, and he could almost taste the icy Popsicle between his lips. Near the curb, he broke away from Carol and was run over by a '49 Olds, a Grey Tudor.

That car was the tornado my grandmother was sure had missed her house.

Eddie didn't die until early evening. His mother and his uncles were with him at the hospital. They watched his tiny lungs lift in the air, ribs and lungs trying to make peace again. They watched his body flutter, like the scales of fish, or butterflies. Then the air stopped, the room lost all its sound, and Eddie was a stone.

My father saw his nephew die.

Just a few days after the funeral, Tom Coyne called a realtor.

CHAPTER 3

I remember having no idea what a *Tudor* was when my parents first started talking about our new house. I heard "two door" and wondered why it was so special—our old house had two doors too. When my parents heard me say this, they laughed and snapped the rubber band on the ponytail that sprouted on the top of my head like a tuft of weeds.

Right before the move, and in the months that followed, we drove west of town several times to see another Tudor house—Harvey's. My dad thought because there was *so much of it* I'd really get the image of what a Tudor was in my head if I saw it. He always loved to teach me things.

"It's a Tudor *man*-sion!" my father would often say, sitting on his sofa rolling out the syllables.

It was *his* sofa, not ours, and more of an *idea* than a piece of furniture, really. Although it wore out and had to be replaced many times, in the most essential ways it stayed the same. The sofa was always long—because Tom Coyne was over six feet tall—and no one ever sat in it but my father. It was tan in the 1950s with nylon upholstery, flowered in the 1960s, bright gold and plush in the 1970s, ruffled homespun in the 1980s. It stayed in the same spot in the living room of our Evergreen Avenue house for nearly fifty years, and it wore out exactly the same way every time, rubbed clean of fabric by my father's bony rear, his palms, the elbow of his right arm that

1548 Evergreen Avenue, 1952

braced his head to line up with the TV. It's where my father spent the last week of his life, and when I sold it in my dad's front yard, it smelled like death.

Right after he said "man-sion," he would rush to his crossword puzzle dictionary (always on the coffee table in front of the sofa) and look up the word. "*Stately,*" he said one time, giving me a synonym he thought I would like, and I did. I still remember learning that word in the living room of my father's house, and learning other words there from Tom Coyne and his crossword puzzle dictionary. That book, and the weekly *Reader's Digest* (always left open on my bed to the vocabulary quiz), were the Great Books—the Harvard Classics—of my early education.

A *stately* house, a *man-sion,* was so important that it always had a name. *A name.* I couldn't believe it.

Harbel Manor. It was formed from the first syllable of Harvey's name and the last syllable of his wife's—Idabelle. I'd never seen a word made from two people's names before, but once I got the idea I asked my dad if we could name *our* new house after the three of *us*—especially since my mother's name, *Annabelle,* was so much like *Idabelle.* Why not call our house *Tombel,* I asked my dad. Or maybe use the first three letters of my name—*Joyce*—and call it *Joybel.* My mother always told me *Joyce* was a happy name. My father was the one who chose it, but not just for its happy sound. It had five letters, just like *Coyne,* our last name, and four of them appeared in both words, and he liked the way *Joyce* and *Coyne* balanced so perfectly on the page, almost like figures on a ledger sheet. I always wanted a name with more syllables that took longer to say and sounded romantic and was mysterious—a name like *Claudia* or *Suzette* or even *Sheral,* with an *S.* Everyone would think I was happy all the time with a name like *Joyce,* and I didn't want them to. Romantic heroines in books weren't *happy*—they cried a lot, went mad sometimes, threw themselves off high cliffs when their lovers left them. My father tried to get me to cheer up by pointing out that *Ann* was my middle name, so I had more to choose from. But *Ann* was just a single syllable too, and all it seemed to do was draw attention to how much *Joyce* and *Coyne* were really like each other, the way an *And* would do. It may as well have been *Joyce And Coyne* or *Joyce 'N Coyne* (like ham 'n eggs), as far as I was concerned.

"No," Dad said when I asked if our house could have a name. "Not for us." I begged my dad to tell me why, but he just shrugged and scratched his great head of hair—*hard,* as if he were trying to pry open his brain. *Not for us,* he said again. Not for the Coynes of Evergreen Avenue.

It shouldn't have surprised me that Harvey Firestone named *his* house. After all, he named everything else. The schools, the banks, the shops, the streets in our community.

We banked at the Firestone Bank, bought life and auto insurance at the Firestone Insurance Agency, shopped at the Firestone Employees Store or the stores on Aster Avenue—the street Harvey set aside for a business district when he built his town. We were members of the Firestone Clubhouse (where I learned to bowl and swim), and I tossed baseballs with my friends at the Firestone Park Stadium, where Harvey's workers played against teams from other plants in the city. On Sunday mornings, most people in the Park attended Firestone Park Presbyterian Church or Firestone Park Methodist Church, both located just a few yards west of the *actual* park at the center of our community, a park with swings and tennis courts, a baseball diamond and a shelter house. Churchgoers would file down my street to the Boulevard on Sunday mornings in long lines, dressed in brown suits and Sunday shoes.

All the kids in Firestone Park went to Firestone Park Elementary School, built on land that Harvey owned, one street east of the park. He had even driven a tractor to help clear the site once construction began.

It wasn't a surprise that Harvey convinced the city to build a school in *his* name on land that *he* donated to Akron. Nor was it a surprise that the building ended up looking like a castle. If Harvey liked houses to look like mansions, of course he would like schools to look like castles. Everything had to be bigger than life and better than average to please him. Firestone Park Elementary School was a medieval castle, and about the only thing it lacked was a moat (though not far from the front entrance there *was* a wading pool for many years). There was even a long row of hedges that fringed the

Wading pool in front of Firestone Park Elementary School, 1925 (Courtesy of Bridgestone/Firestone, Inc.)

street the school was on when I was there, as prickly as a stockade.

Unlike many things about Firestone Park I *didn't* notice when I was a girl, I *did* notice that my school looked like a castle. I may not have had all the right names for the parts back then, but I knew the general shape of things. My cousin Paul and I had assembled a large cardboard castle together in his attic, the kind with a big guardhouse and battlement in the front and turrets in the back, and we knew how things locked in place and how they were supposed to fit. We had spent many hours knocking each other's knights off pitched roofs, staircases, and high towers. On our trips to Florida together, we visited Fort Marion in St. Augustine and on the tops of its walls

Author at Fort Marion in St. Augustine, Florida

saw the same kind of parapet that was on our cardboard castle *and* our elementary school—with all those indentations for firing cannon balls. I have a picture of myself standing by a cannon that pokes through one of those cuts in the wall, called a *crenel.*

Our school had five-sided turrets by the front entrance and merlons and crenels cut clear across its false battlement. I heard heralds with long brass trumpets playing fanfares in the morning and saw knights jousting on the playground in the afternoon. I imagined myself climbing on the roof and pouring boiling oil on the heads of invading seventh graders from the junior high.

A six-foot painting of Harvey Firestone hung on one wall of the entranceway, right across from a painting of George Washington about the same size. The men were equal in my mind. The only difference was George's powdered wig, and I think I always knew that Harvey could have had one of those too, if he'd wanted.

Harvey *always* liked being at the center of things, so the painting and the school and the statue seemed right, somehow. He was even at the controls of the first streetcar that screeched its way into Firestone Park during World War I, after he insisted that the city extend the streetcar route to the Park's business district. There was a terrible flu epidemic at the time (it actually killed some of my Akron relatives), but Harvey ignored an edict from the Health Department that warned people to avoid crowds. With pride and perfect confidence that illness would never dare come close to him, he glided right down Aster in that tight little car, right to the front of the first stores built on the street, right in the middle of a major war and a major epidemic.

That was Harvey for you.

❧❧❧

On the way out to Harbel Manor, my dad would tell me stories about Harvey's polo fields, fox hunts, and the herds of Holsteins and sheep he had brought from his boyhood homestead in Columbiana County. Nothing but the house was there in 1952, of course. Idabelle still resided at Harbel Manor part of the year, but Harvey had died in 1938 and the sheep had gone baaing back to their Columbiana home.

My dad was right. Harbel Manor *did* look like our house. Well, sort of. It looked like our house doubled, then tripled, then quadrupled in size, and multiplied once more. It was like the paper dolls I used to cut and then unfold. Our house would be like *one* of the dolls standing in the row. One very *small* doll in one very long row about the length of a city block.

Harbel Manor (Courtesy of Bridgestone/Firestone, Inc.)

Dad always kept magnifying glasses close by. You'd find them on the coffee table, in his pockets, in kitchen bowls. They crawled under the cushions of his sofa, maybe needing a rest from my dad. A childhood illness had caused my father to lose most of his sight in his right eye, so he often held a lens over things he was looking at. He used the image of that glass whenever he tried to explain hard things to me.

"Harvey's place," he'd say, "is just like our house—only through a glass." I took the magnifying glass in my hand—two lenses folded out of it—and nodded my head, and saw our little Tudor begin to swell into the house where Harvey had once lived, and where for a long, long time I pretended he still did.

∾≈∾

Brick and stucco, oak trim, drop stair access to an unfinished attic area used for storage, textured ceiling. Seventy-one years old, on a pie-shaped lot. Subject is a well-built and well-main-

tained home of better than average quality. Good curb appeal. Recent improvements include newer furnace, C/A, copper plumbing. New wiring with 100 AMP breaker box and some newer carpets. Front hall entry and attractive oak woodwork, as well as a wood burning fireplace in the living room. Second level includes three bedrooms and full bath as well as small den/powder room. Irregular site of 7200 square feet. Topography mostly level, and drainage appears to be adequate. Census tract 5047. Well-regarded area of south Akron at the corner of Evergreen and Crescent. Nicely landscaped. Taxes $897.28.

That's the way the appraiser described our Tudor house nine months after my father died and I put it up for sale. That's everything it was. Not a home like Harvey's. It was a Tudor Revival—one of the plans Harvey approved for houses constructed in Firestone Park during the second wave of building. He liked to see his reflection everywhere, I guess, even in the homes he sold to his workers. But, of course, it wasn't much like Harbel Manor. I don't think Harbel had a breakfast nook or a bathroom you could barely turn around in.

And yet, if the house had been twice as big—three times, *four*—if it had sat on the highest hill in all of Akron, had great halls and game rooms, chandeliers and fountains, barns and pastures, tapestries and angels on the wall, Limoges pitchers and fine porcelain plates in cherry cabinets, outbuildings and gardens everywhere, it could not have been more to me than it was.

I've mined that little house a thousand times. And every time I return to it, there's a new corner, a new room, a whole wing I've never seen before.

In some odd way, it is even bigger than the house where Harvey lived.

CHAPTER 4

❦❦❦

My dad was a Catholic, but not the churchgoing kind. Sunday mornings he would lie on the sofa in his underwear and shave his whiskers with his Norelco, reading the *Akron Beacon Journal* from cover to cover. My father loved the news, and I can't think of him without hearing a radio in the background or seeing him on that sofa turning pages of newsprint on lazy Sunday mornings.

I'd wave to him when I left the house, though my mother was usually busy finding the church envelope and didn't have time for a formal leave-taking. Sometimes she managed a simple, "Bye, Tommy," but always with her back halfway out the door, her head pointing sharply toward our car, her keys swinging in one hand and the church envelope folded in the other, thick with dollar bills.

My mother and I seldom missed a Sunday at the Lutheran church in Goosetown where my parents were married. When my mother was a girl, the German Lutherans in Goosetown met at a small church that stood on East Thornton Street, right behind the Haberkost house on Grant. In 1927 a new church, a huge Gothic monster, was dedicated a few blocks south.

We'd pick up several of my mother's sisters on our way. There were four of them—five Haberkost daughters in all, counting Annabelle. A carload of Haberkost women going off to church was a normal part of the week for me. I liked the way it felt, and their high, chirpy voices made me think of parakeets.

Author and Annabelle Coyne, Sunday morning

❦❦❦

I always had a parakeet. Well, after our dog died. The family story was that one night our dog chased a burglar out of our Goosetown house, and the story kept growing each time my parents told it until they had that little dog—a thing about the size of a grasshopper—attacking the ankle of a man with a shotgun who was trying to kidnap me in a burlap bag. I remember being jealous of our dog Rusty after his brave act because my parents kept tying little ribbons around the fur on his head and he started to look a little like me— and get the attention *I* preferred for myself. But before the month of the attempted robbery—or kidnapping, whatever it was—had ended, so had the dog's life. One day he just started whirling in smaller and smaller circles on the kitchen linoleum, until he collapsed and died. Maybe all that glory had just gone to his head. This happened right before the move, and I remember not feeling quite as sad as I probably should have.

We buried the little dog in the backyard, and after a service I conducted—with Bible verses and everything (I often told my friend from the Akron Baptist Temple about it)—my dad took me to the pet store and let me choose the dog's successor.

I chose a parakeet. We never had a dog again, even though my dad talked about poodles a lot.

I always loved things that flew. Kites, butterflies, and especially the Goodyear blimp. Firestone was *my* company, there was no doubt of that. But I was always a little disappointed—maybe jealous—that we never had a Firestone blimp or a hangar to keep it in. A blimp my cousins and I could watch and wave to when we rode our bikes up and down the streets of Firestone Park. My uncle Paul *had* sung at the dedication of the *USS Akron* in 1931, built by Goodyear-Zeppelin, so the Goodyear blimp had always had a *small* connection to our family, even though the *Akron* itself was blown into the sea two years after my uncle sang for it and seventy-three of its seventy-six crew members were killed. But even if the *Akron* itself had flown in the skies when we were young, it never would have felt quite like *ours*.

We bought green birds at first because they cost less, but when my dad started getting good raises we bought blue ones for a few dollars more. My best birds were always blue. A blue parakeet, for one thing, could be trained to go to the bathroom. That's how we described this strange ability of our birds (well, the *blue* ones, never the green or yellow) to somehow figure out how to put their droppings on a piece of plastic spread across the dining-room table rather than on a lampshade or a human shoulder.

It didn't *always* work. One time around my dad's birthday a bald insurance agent came to our house and our bird perched right on top of the man's shiny head. The bird slid around on that slick surface for a few seconds and then flew off, but not before he left a warm dropping that rolled down the agent's forehead and into one eye. I remember thinking how funny it was that my bird was trying to perch on something shaped like the ostrich egg we'd seen in school.

My cousins owned parakeets too. Once my aunt Ruth forgot a bird was on her shoulder when she went outside, and when she leaned over for a clothespin, the wind pushed under the bird's wings and sent him on his way. Perky traveled clear to Kenmore, several miles from his Ivy Place house. He flew onto the porch of a nice family and waited on a wicker chair for the first shoulder to emerge in the morning, flew all that way as if he had a road map on the underside of his wings and knew his destination. We placed an ad in the paper (my uncle Paul even let us kids write it, thinking, I'm sure, that it didn't much matter *who* wrote it because the bird was dead) and recovered the poor thing.

Everyone in Firestone Park said it was a miracle. I normally didn't believe in miracles, even though I knew some Bible stories about them. Healing lepers, splitting the Red Sea right down the middle, turning one small fish into enough food to feed a population about as big as Summit County—these things sounded pretty impossible to me, even as a child. I guess it shouldn't surprise me that my friend with the Buster Brown haircut could smell doubt all over me, even then. But Perky was real, and Perky *was* a miracle. He was lost, but his instincts went with him, all the way to Kenmore. Maybe a little luck was involved—there could have been a lightning storm instead of the light rain that fell the day he flew away, I suppose. But, I decided, Perky was mainly a miracle. If I could understand Perky, I knew I would live a long, long time.

My aunts not only *sounded* like my birds, but Sunday mornings they *looked* like them too. Their hats, especially. They all wore tiny felt hats with small veils in front and huge plumes shooting out the back in lime green, blue, yellow. Feathers bobbed as they talked all at once, and cooed. There was never silence, the way there was when a man spoke in a car and you felt you had to listen.

"Can you believe the summer heat!"

"*What* sale at O'Neil's?"

Their favorite subject, though, was a certain majorette and a French horn player in the high-school band. My mom would pick up one aunt, then another, and before they had both feet in the car each one would start up about that poor majorette. Her skirts were too short, her hair too blond, blouses too low. If she didn't watch herself, they said, she'd have *one in the oven* and the French horn player would be packing up his instrument and heading out of town in the middle of the night.

"If I ever see *you* kiss a boy that way—" they said, staring straight at me, their eyes as big as Stop signs.

They never told me what they'd do, but I knew it wouldn't be good. I imagined them hooking my lips together with yarn and a crochet needle, or jumping in the middle of the kiss and pulling me home by my eyelids. I always knew that majorettes were in a lot more danger than I ever was, so I never understood why my aunts compared me to them. I was in *band,* too clumsy to ever be a majorette. What boy in his right mind would want to look at a girl dressed in band pants, gloves, a hard sixteen-inch hat with a silly white plume floating out the back, and a clarinet stuck in her mouth, when he could look at a majorette in a short skirt? After every band show, my lower lip bore the permanent impression of a reed. It didn't even look like a lip anymore. Only majorettes had full lips as firm and plump as nectarines. There wasn't much danger of the dark, sexy French horn player coming after me.

While my mother drove and my aunts talked, the windows were always rolled up, until the air in our Hudson became everything Akron air was not. Sweet smells were everywhere. Lily of the Valley floated from the driver's seat—my mother's smell. Aunt Marie worked at the cosmetic counter of O'Neil's Department Store, and I always shoved and pushed to get to sit next to her in the back seat. She sold Evening in Paris perfume and I loved its odor. "Soir de Paris," she would say with a south Akron accent. "'The Most Famous Fragrance in the World'—made by Bourjois," she would say, as if I were a customer at her counter looking for a Christmas gift. Sometimes she brought little blue vials of it home for us to try, and I'd douse it behind my ears, look through the cobalt blue glass, and imagine what it would be like to be as pretty as my aunt Marie, or to be French and smell good all the time.

I grew up thinking that church was something only women did. In some ways the inside of that car on Sunday mornings remains one of the safest, sweetest places in my memory, in spite of my aunts' warnings about kissing, which were really warnings about sex. I selfishly liked it that my dad didn't go with us, even though he really was my best friend back then.

I *know* my aunts liked not having him there too, but sometimes they called him a *sinner* for not going along with us. I knew he wasn't perfect, but I didn't like thinking of my dad as a *sinner*, because I knew full well what happened to *them*. Our minister saw the world

The Haberkost sisters

as filled with saints and sinners. He taught his congregation, including the Haberkosts, that only Christians could be saved. My dad was obviously no saint, and not a Christian in the churchgoing way, so he was pretty much doomed in a lot of people's eyes. It seemed unfair to me, and I didn't like knowing he would burn in hell, but that's what our minister said would happen in the end to unbelievers like Tom Coyne.

Our Sunday school teachers said it too. I remember one story a woman with bright red hair told us while she wept. She had just come home from a trip to North Carolina with her husband. Driving late one night, they had gotten lost and had somehow ended up on a dirt road. There were no lights except their headlights, no landmarks of any sort, but for some strange reason her husband suddenly jammed on the brakes, causing his wife and him to jolt close to the windshield. He got out and found that his front tires were perched on the edge of a cliff.

"It was Jesus Christ," our red-haired teacher told us. If they hadn't taken Christ along with them, they would be at the bottom of a huge ravine right now, she said. Flattened. I admit that after that I worried even more about my father's bad driving than I usually did. He had poor eyesight, poor instincts, turned too sharp and stopped too fast, and without Christ, I began to think, we didn't have a chance.

I loved the gossip of my aunts, though, even when my dad was at its center. There were no pirates or sea captains sailing through the Park. Once in a while there was a fight at the shelter house over a girl (not me, of course), but little action to speak of in our neighborhood. One friend from high school said she was going to run away and join the circus, but I don't think she ever did. Another friend had a pretty mother who worked at Polsky's. Everyone said she was a call girl. Our high school *did* host a brief visit for Ladybird Johnson in September of 1964. She walked around in a linen dress and pearls and shook hands in the parking lot. It was raining and she wore one of those foldup plastic rain hats and the principal ran after her, trying to keep her dry with his umbrella. She met our class president, said a few words at a microphone set up for her, received a bouquet of mums, waved farewell to a huge crowd, and then disappeared in a small caravan of cars. It was one of the most exciting things I remember ever happening in Akron.

No, it was my *aunts* who drew the weapons—and the battle lines—in my life. *My* source of adventure. I loved their stories, even when I doubted them, and even when they made me mad.

Communion Sunday was a familiar scene in the ongoing Haberkost drama. My mother and my aunts were raised to believe that you couldn't take communion if you couldn't forgive somebody for something they had done. So if anything was festering inside a Haberkost woman on a communion Sunday, they sat firm and stared straight ahead of them when the usher called their row to the bread and wine at the altar rail (no timid grape juice for Lutherans, which somehow made me think I needed to be a lot stronger than I knew I really was). Communion was served once a month in our synod, and it often coincided with my periods. Nearly every communion Sunday it seemed like I woke up with cramps. The distant blood and body of Christ were easier for me to imagine when I walked toward that silver cup spilling blood of my own—and somehow the stories of my angry aunts were easier to imagine too.

On more than one communion Sunday, a Haberkost woman would just drop her head, like the statue in front of us of Christ bolted to the cross. I could almost hear it fall, heavy and sharp as an ax. When the usher tapped the edge of our pew, the rest of us would rise, brace our hands on the seat ahead of us, arch our backs, and glide like half moons past the human form behind us that felt as brittle as rock.

Not taking communion was a way that a silent message could be delivered, or a sentence carried out. For me there was a kind of excitement in imagining what was wrong if someone in our family kept her seat. What had someone done? Or *forgotten* to do? What hurtful words had escaped a sister's lips? Whose husband had disappointed one of them? Who was jealous of whom, and for what? Who was playing the martyr now, and what price would be exacted? I seldom understood those scenes I saw unfold, but I imagined everything about them.

It seemed to me that my aunts were even harder on my boyfriends than they were on each other, or on the men in *their* lives. Especially on the boy from church they *knew* I really liked. I understand the severity of my aunts now, because I've seen it in myself.

I've become a mother, like most of them, and know the kind of worry only mothers know. I know mistakes in love can set the world on a deadly course, and you can never take them back. Not through divorce, not through forgiveness, not ever, not in any way. I've felt worry that has made me act like people I hate, and say horrible things I never can call back.

In their minds, I'm sure my aunts saw me pregnant with this boy's child, saw my youth—*their* youth—slip away in one fierce kiss. They probably never hated him at all, the way I thought they did. He wasn't even *real* to them. What they hated was his power to touch my imagination and take away all the hope they had placed there, through their gifts of daily love, Campbell's alphabet soup, vials of perfume. His lust was an assault on me, *and* on them.

I had fallen in love on a church hayride. The boy I loved was not a *nice* boy, my aunts told me, even in the beginning when I'd just drop his name now and then to test things out. Their voices fell an octave when they told me the boy I liked—no, *loved*, I told myself, I *loved* this boy—was not a *nice* boy. He smelled like cigarettes and had a ducktail. But no one *else* wanted to kiss me, no one else ever tried to make my lips feel the way the majorette's felt *all the time*. Just saying his name gave me goose bumps. It hurt to hear that the only boy in the world who knew I was alive was not good enough for me. Our relationship consisted of occasional phone calls, with sappy Bobby Vinton songs playing in the background, and a single kiss on a pile of wet hay on a hot summer night in a farmer's field where a mall now stands.

The things my aunts hated about him were the very things I liked. He smoked in a private, romantic way—outside in the angles of the church, with his hands cupped around his cigarette, and his collar up. His wonderful brown ducktail made me think he was a bird about to take flight, something that understood air and lived in it entirely. And that motorcycle that made my aunts' eyes grow wide and their lips knot when he revved it up made me, for the first time in my life, want to leave this place I loved, leave my aunts and mother and all of it behind, and ride away. I looked at the motorcycle, stared at that metal motor, the seat, the thick handlebars and fancy pedals. The bike looked like an insect to me, all segments and body parts. As I stared harder, and longer, it took the shape of a boy. It was as if I were looking right inside a boy at his bones and organs and everything.

The bike, and the boy, found a telephone pole one night. My young lover impaled himself on one of those spiked footsteps repairmen used. He'd called me that night and teased me about sneaking out with him. I didn't go, I didn't even know if he really wanted me to, but if I had, if I had ridden into the night on the back of his bike, placed my arms around his slender waist, the same spike that took his life would have skewered me to him for all eternity.

"He was a *wild* boy, Joyce," my aunts said, trying to comfort me, perhaps suspecting that I was thinking not only of the boy, but of my own reckless heart. They'd traded *not nice* for *wild*, coming closer to the word they'd really wanted all along.

"He was bound for hell," they added. "Forget him now."

But they didn't stop there. They knew I needed time to learn how women saw the world before men arrived in it to change it forever. They knew they had to frighten me to try to keep me safe, to keep that spike a wide distance from my young flesh.

He was born out of wedlock, they finally whispered. *He was a bastard*. There was a rumor going around that this boy was born to a man not his father while his *real* father was off at war. That's why he was so mixed up. So crazy and wild. His mother had done this terrible thing, and there was no hope for the boy.

I'd never heard the word *bastard* before, and I didn't know where to keep a word like that. It made me fear not only the boy who had died, but everything else too. I felt unclean. I had let a *bastard* kiss me, tempt me toward Death itself, so what did that make *me*?

I was not strong enough for wine, not strong enough for anything.

I felt *I* was going to hell too—or worse—after what my aunts said about the boy from church who died all alone on a country road.

❧❧

But I never *really* felt *my dad* was going to hell—the way people said he would because he stayed away from church. Dad didn't worship *God*, exactly, it was true. He worshipped his *company*. His faith seemed as real to me as anything the Lutherans professed. People at the church were always talking about giving their life to Christ, but I never really felt they meant it the way my dad did. He gave his life every single day. To Harvey Firestone.

Sundays were a time of celebration for my father too. Right after my mother and I returned from church, Dad took me on a weekly pilgrimage to Harvey Firestone's statue. We may as well have carried a hymnal under our arms and worn choir robes. No one at the church loved Jesus the way my dad and I loved Harvey Firestone. Members plopped down in their pews and nodded off when the thick air of summer pressed through the low windows of the sanctuary and made their hearts beat hard and slow. For my dad and me, our blood moved faster as we walked down Sage, then through the meadows and woods that led to the back of Harvey's statue. As we got closer, Dad sometimes picked me up by both arms and said to close my eyes, *we'd fly*. We were moving that fast.

I liked going to the statue a lot better than sitting in the Goose-town church. I liked Jesus all right then, but I *loved* the statue of Harvey Firestone from the first time I saw it on the way to our new house. I loved Harvey in part, I suppose, because I could feel that my *dad* loved him almost more than anything.

We began our worship service by reading the huge sentence that wrapped around the granite seat behind Harvey's statue. Tom Coyne stretched his long arm, pointed like a conductor, cleared his giant voice, and cued me to join in when it was time. His white shirt was open at the collar, his sleeves rolled up, a string tie with a bucking horse medallion around his neck. I liked the silver horse more than the knots on the long ties Dad had to wear to work. He never got the knots quite slim enough, and they often looked like the noose I drew when I played Hangman.

We started walking from left to right, following the huge sentence to its end. *He believed what the centuries said,* we read, almost to the middle of the seat now, *as against the years and as against the hours.*

"What's that mean?" I would ask.

"It means we're safe here, honey," my dad would say, completely unaware that the Park was *anything* but safe for the Tom Coynes. "A century is a hundred years, you know, and this statue and the stone and all those factories, well—." He stopped to think about what he had said. "It's, uh, like the Roman Empire." That's how he always summed up important things. *It was like the Roman Empire.*

And then he cupped his hands together as if there were a small bird inside, or a pair of dice, just the way the minister folded *his* hands at the Lutheran church when he moved from the pulpit to the altar rail in his long, dark robe.

I really wasn't paying attention while my father spoke. I was busy looking at the carvings of naked gods and goddesses in the granite along the back of the seat. I thought their bodies were beautiful and I wanted to touch them, but I knew my dad might not like that. Even then I could tell some parts were missing. You could see the muscles

Harvey S. Firestone Memorial, showing statue and exedra
(Courtesy of Bridgestone/Firestone, Inc.)

in their arms and thighs and abdomens, but they either had their legs conveniently crossed or their hips contorted so severely that the parts of the anatomy that interested me most remained hidden, no matter how hard I looked for them. I tried to imagine the missing parts growing from the stones, but it took time to do this, and my father usually had moved us to the front of Harvey's throne before I had everything in place.

We stood in front of the tall pedestal that lifted Harvey Firestone high into the air. It was really a *chair* that Harvey sat in, not a throne, my dad reminded me, the same way he always told me the statue was *bronze*, not gold. He would walk me to the back of the statue and show me the straight lines of the chair. I'd agree with him and nod.

The seat was, after all, shaped a little like the chair my grandfather Coyne sat in to watch TV. Mr. Firestone's chair didn't have maroon upholstery and arms worn slick as oil, like W. T. Coyne's chair, but everything else was the same. Mr. Firestone even rested his arms and hands the way W. T. Coyne sometimes did when I sat with him on Saturday nights to watch men hit each other on *The Fight of the Week.*

I saw it was a chair, but I *knew* it was a throne.

When I looked up, bending my skinny neck like a Flex-Straw, Mr. Firestone seemed to be trying to reach down and grab me. He was slumped forward slightly, as if he had a message he wanted to whisper in my ear but I wasn't close enough to hear it. My dad, who had already taught me how to climb the small apple tree in our back-yard, picked me up by my waist and lifted me over Mr. Firestone's left knee.

I knew what to do next. I would grab the thumb of Mr. Fire-stone's left hand and wriggle into his lap. His other hand, draped over his right leg, formed an iron gate and prevented me from falling.

If someone were standing on South Main Street and happened to look across the wide lawn at the statue on almost any Sunday af-ternoon in the early 1950s, they would have seen a swatch of red fab-ric, four struggling bony limbs, and a white shock of hair shooting straight out the top of a small head.

I loved everything about the Firestone statue. The feel of hot metal and sun on my bare legs, the kingly folds of bronze fabric that my imagination turned to gold. The way my dad boosted me into Harvey's lap and sometimes coupled his final push with the secret words, *Clark Gable worked for Firestone, dear Ann.*

Clark Gable, Europe, and Harvey Firestone were mixed up in my mind for a long time because my dad always said their names in a single breath. They were the three most famous things in the world to him. His Holy Trinity. *You see things like this in Europe,* he'd say about the statue sometimes. Of course I believed him, even though he'd never been to Europe.

Nor would he ever go.

All children have a favorite view that returns to them in memory, sometimes just at the moment when they're on the verge of being old. For some it's the view of the ocean from a giant rock on a beach, of a private street seen through a crack in an attic window, of a train winding out of town. For others, it's a bridge that crosses a shallow creek somewhere in the woods, a tree with cherries so sour and so good that you can't sort the pleasure out from the pain, a crack in a bedroom door that lets the secrets of adults begin to filter in and crease your skin.

For me it was that view from Harvey's lap, the panoramic glimpse of the Firestone empire that greeted me from my bronze perch on that high summit.

No one laughed at Akron in the 1950s. It was the Rubber Capital of the World, and people who lived there refused to see that it had already begun to change.

There *was* no better view than the one I had.

To Begin with,
They Looked Alike . . .

❧❧❧

The original Dedication of the statue took place in 1950. It was a big event. Even Life Magazine *came to town to cover the story.*

My grandfather was there.

A souvenir was mailed out to Firestone employees by Harvey S. Firestone Jr. a year after the ceremony. It's illustrated with pictures from the occasion—the Dedication itself, the Exposition of Historical and Product Displays held in the Research Building, the Ringling Brothers and Barnum & Bailey Circus that the company hired to entertain 37,000 employees and their family members under its Big Top.

One of the strangest pictures in the program is of two elephants. Well, one gigantic elephant and one very small dog dressed up to look like an elephant. The elephant and the small dog both have blankets draped over their backs. On the elephant's blanket are the words, "Firestone 1950." Tied to the dog's back is a small cloth the size of a large napkin, and it reads, "Firestone 1900."

With my father's magnifying glass, I've found two pictures of W. T. in the souvenir book, but none of my dad. I think my dad was present too, but I can't prove it. Where else would T. W. Coyne have been on a day like this?

W. T. Coyne always looked as if he belonged in a Firestone ad, and the souvenir photos are no exception. In one photo he's standing with some other executives from subsidiary plants, his hands folded behind his back, as if he's trying to balance the weight of his heavy stomach. Displaying something between reverence and smug complacency, he's looking at a fifty-six-inch All Non-Skid Sky Champion Airplane Tire.

He's in the sixth row in the second picture. You can tell he's happy to be in this shot, even though he's buried toward the back. He's made sure that his large head is visible to the camera, and he's smiling wide. The photograph was taken right in front of Harbel Manor, where Harvey Sr. used to hold important meetings with his executives. The Fiftieth Anniversary Committee thought it would be a good idea to revive the Harbel Manor tradition with a buffet lunch and a leisurely stroll of the grounds.

Whenever I visited my grandfather, it was the person in the Dedication program who always greeted me. The comptroller of Firestone subsidiary plants. I never saw him in anything other than a white shirt. Unlike my dad, he never rolled his sleeves up, even on days when hot Ohio summers cooked his brick bungalow and his Firestone thermometer hit triple digits. He walked the rooms of his Reed Avenue house in Firestone Park with his hands clasped behind him, dressed in those hot shirts, just waiting for someone to ask him to add things up.

CHAPTER 5

❧❧

People always said W. T. and T. W. were a lot alike. It's easy to understand why they would say this. To begin with, they looked alike. Dad's hair was just like his father's—so curly and thick you couldn't see his skull. He tried hard to act like him, too, but that wasn't quite as easy.

T. W. told old stories, just the way his dad did, but they didn't start—and they certainly didn't end—like Grandpa's. Their stories were like chapters from different books. Even though I knew their relatives were all the same and everything they said should fit together, I couldn't line things up.

My father talked about *coal* all the time, but my grandfather always remained silent on the subject. Even though he'd worked in Pennsylvania mines before he came to Rubber Town, I never heard my grandfather mention his former life or the mineral that braided through the hills of his past. He told *great* stories, don't get me wrong. But they were usually about fighters like Sugar Ray Robinson and Rocky Marciano, or about John McGraw, who managed the New York Giants.

No one was greater in my grandpa's eyes than John McGraw, because Grandpa always said McGraw was related to us. I didn't realize for years that if he was (and I'm not sure of this), it must have been through Bessie McGraw, Grandpa's wife, not through W. T. Nine times McGraw took the Giants to the World Series, Grandpa said. *Nine times,* he repeated, as slowly as his tongue would go. W. T. called McGraw "Little Napoleon," a name he said everyone used for the man. He said it with such affection that I remember how surprised I was when I learned much later that Napoleon stole whole countries (*and* their treasures) and killed hundreds of thousands of people who stood in his way.

My dad often showed me pieces of coal he had brought to Akron after he left Scranton. Tom Coyne had worked as a breaker boy before he moved to Akron, just like other males in his family when they were young. The pieces of anthracite coal he carried with him were the very chunks he had sorted sitting in a Pennsylvania mine.

Coal always seemed impenetrable to me—black and dense—but to my dad, it was a crystal ball and made the past return whenever he looked at it.

He would talk about lives that began across the ocean when he stared at those lumps, each surface as clear to him as the face of a relative. My great-grandfather, he told me, just packed up and left the mines in Manchester, England. Left behind all the deaths and falling roofs and gas explosions and strikes and blackened lungs and poverty. Just sailed away. He landed in New York and then traveled to Pennsylvania to find work. He bored holes into American coal instead of English—prepared the powder for the blast—watched black mineral shatter into fuel and money for other people.

Years later, William, his son and my grandfather, left the Pennsylvania mines his father had thought would make a better life, and traveled to the Rubber Capital of the World.

When Dad told me how coal formed and how his family took tons of it from the Pennsylvania mountainsides, I began to look for it everywhere. I would dig down farther and farther with my father's foldup army shovel. China was less interesting to me than coal, so

Bessie, T. W., W. T., and Mildred Coyne, newly arrived in Akron
from Pennsylvania

when people asked me if I was digging to China, I always said no. China had no stories that were relevant to me, as far as I could tell. But coal did. Every time my father talked about a piece of coal, the stories came. Stories and coal were one thing to me. Coal was dangerous, a place where there was fire and death, a place you needed to ride away from to keep your children safe. Coal shined like a black mirror and you saw the dark, scary side of life when you looked in it.

"Your eyes get hard if you stare at it too long," my father warned me. But his sad stories, edged with danger, were the ones that I liked best.

I'd work until I heard the shovel hit something hard, and then pretend it was coal, even though the rock I struck looked nothing at all like the samples my father let me hold.

"It's coal!" I would run and tell him.

"It might be," he'd say.

And then I'd invent a story about a breaker boy who held this *very* chunk of coal a long, long time ago (in a mine I'd never find except in the story I would tell) and ground its point into the head of an angry snake—a rattler or a copperhead—and saved his family from great harm.

◈◈◈

My grandfather tried to forget his coal mining past. My father wanted to remember. That somehow has come to be an important distinction in my mind. In some odd way, I know it may have been the most important difference between my father and his dad.

They seemed so much alike when they were talking about Firestone. If you didn't know about the coal, you really could confuse the two. Firestone was the story they had in common, and it took up a lot of space. My dad wanted a bright future with the company so much that sometimes I felt he was studying his dad to find out how to get it.

"A *comptroller*," my father said over and over in the 1950s when he talked about W. T. He would shake his head, just the way W. T. did.

"Mmm, mmm," he would say, his lips humming and that head moving from side to side.

I could only guess that Grandpa Coyne's careful avoidance of the subject of coal had something to do with that word *comptroller*. Like other big words my father used, I didn't understand what he was saying for a long time. I thought he'd said *controller* (some people pronounce the word that way, and maybe that's how Tom Coyne said it too), and that always seemed to fit my grandpa perfectly, so I never asked my father what the word really meant until I was older.

Knows his numbers, everyone said about W. T., and that's what eventually landed him his job as a Firestone executive. I didn't know there was a relationship between the word *comptroller* and my grandpa's gift with numbers, but I certainly recognized that he counted better than anyone else I'd ever known. Even better than my teachers.

I often wonder when W. T. first realized that he was a wizard with numbers. He may have figured it out as a breaker boy himself. What games did he invent with pea coal and walnut coal, the black beads on *his* abacus? When did he first notice that the piles he built with his coal were remarkable? When did he first slide down the log he sat on, away from the other boys, separating himself forever from the life that they would lead?

Numbers were his ticket out of the mines. He would return to Pennsylvania in the 1940s, but only to work as an executive at Firestone's Pottstown plant, not to look at the coal he had fled. *Never* to look at the coal again.

People say you can't count what a relationship is worth. But I can. Every time I visited my grandpa, *every single time,* we would add things up. I remember how many bricks were in his fireplace, the dimensions of his kitchen, the number of square feet in each of his closets, the angle of the wooden slats on his garden trellis, the length of his living room and of the long mirror behind his buffet. Time was measured with rulers in my grandpa's house.

As soon as he opened the door of his Reed Avenue house in Firestone Park, he asked me for a number, the way a fortune-teller might.

"What number today, Penny?"

Grandpa Coyne loved to call me by my nickname. He thought it was hilarious that I was *Penny* Coyne, and sometimes would say my name out of the blue, howling in his seat.

Whatever number I would give him, he quickly would divide it by five, or eight, and work the problem out to tenths and hundredths. He taught me fractions, explained graphs, and let me pull his slide rule from its scuffed leather case.

Grandpa was as fast as the adding machine my mother sometimes brought home from work. And he knew it.

I would write the biggest, longest number I could think of on a piece of paper and he would remember it. He could recite a phone number backwards. He taught me chess, but our games were always short because he always won. I would watch his fingers curl on his hands as he thought about each move, then open like pincers on the lobsters we looked at in tanks at Iacomini's Restaurant. I would stare at the yellow callus on his middle finger, from his cigarettes, and his thick, square nails, with great half moons. Sometimes those hands would slip into his pockets and find some shiny change for me, which he always made me count before he placed it in my hand.

On holidays and birthdays there was more than change. He gave gifts of money. Grandpa bought me fifty- and hundred-dollar savings bonds at Christmastime. My grandma Haberkost gave dollar bills. Grandpa Coyne was generous to me, but I could tell the bonds always made my father feel bad. Grandpa made sure his gifts were opened *last,* and liked to see our eyes pop out. It made him laugh, and his stomach move. He liked to be my own Daddy Warbucks, my very own Santa Claus.

W. T. Coyne and Bessie always look happy in old photographs. My grandpa had a good job with Firestone from the day he started

W. T. Coyne, left, receiving twenty-year watch

working for the company. He was going somewhere. He could feel it, his wife could feel it, and his children knew it too.

I have one picture of W. T. receiving his twenty-year watch in his office at a Firestone bomb-loading plant in Fremont, Nebraska. He can't take his eyes off the Elgin pocket watch he's just been given, a watch that I own now. Maybe he was looking at the decorative fleur-de-lis on the back, or his initials, or the gold case. He stands there with two other smiling men, surrounded by mahogany furniture and pictures of soldiers and flags on the walls, and of the Firestone brothers at company plant openings across the nation. In this shot, and others, W. T. wears an expensive suit. You can see the close weave of the fabric, the starched cuffs of his white shirt peeking out from his coat sleeves.

There was never a spot of Pennsylvania coal dust on *those* sleeves, nor a smudge of rubber. My grandfather looked like a croupier in a fancy Las Vegas hotel, someone about to deal a hand of cards or drag a pile of chips toward him with the perfect nails of his clean, white hands.

≈≈≈

T. W. always—*always*—lived in the shadow of W. T. His father was such a big man with the company that I don't think T. W. really ever imagined doing *better* than his father had done. Being his father's shadow was plenty for him.

There is a photo of Tom Coyne taken the day he began his employment with the Firestone Tire & Rubber Company in 1936. For years and years Firestone had a custom of photographing each new employee, and my father is standing on a stage with his name written on a chalkboard perched by his feet.

My father had acne then. In the picture there are streaks of it across his cheeks. He was *that* young. His hair is greased back and he has his glasses off. You can see his slow right eye rolling in, searching like a metal ball in a pinball machine for a place to rest. He has on a dark pinstriped suit, but it looks at least one size too small. A pocket is bulging out, the top button of his double-breasted coat is much too tight, his pants are too long. He's standing too far to the right—way off center. Even the knot in his tie curves to the right, as if an invisible line is yanking it toward the edge, like a leash, and if he leaned just a little more, he might disappear from the camera's view.

His shoes are shined. He always shined his shoes. Grandpa said that shined shoes were the first thing your boss noticed, and my father polished his every night. My dad told me this, and I remember

Company picture of T. W. Coyne, 1936
(Courtesy of Bridgestone/Firestone, Inc.)

pressing white polish into my white bucks with a tiny sponge. I remember bottle after bottle of polish and a terrible fear of a black streak. Sometimes I'd see my dad wipe the dirt and dust from the toes of his shoes with his handkerchief right before he entered his father's house.

In a mirror, the initials T. W. become W. T. Sometimes I wonder if my father knew that. But no matter how my father dressed or shined his shoes, he only fooled himself—the way the mirror did—if he thought he'd one day be the man his father was. I can't know what dreams and hopes were in my father's head the day he posed for his first Firestone picture, his arms dangling awkwardly at his sides, like a puppet on twisted strings. But I think he wanted more than anything to look the way his father did in a suit, and be invited to Harvey's house with other important men.

T. W. always called W. T. *father*—even in the years after the old man died. It was always *Father this* and *Father that.* It made me feel like I was in church sometimes to be with the two of them. In the Reed Avenue house it was always *Father* and *Son*, never *Dad* and *Tommy.* Dad spoke slowly when he visited W. T., as if he were breathing through heavy air and about to choke, his posture improved the second he knocked on W. T.'s door, and inside he seldom smiled, at least not the same way he did at my mom and me. Sometimes, when the conversation stopped, my father bit his nails. W. T. Coyne was, after all, a Firestone executive, a man who had been recruited by Harvey Firestone Sr. himself and deserved respect, and it was hard for my dad to be around a man like that and measure up, or even know how to act.

I *know* that my grandfather's career was something my father wanted too. I'm sure he often thought about it. How could he not? W. T. was reaping the benefits, especially after he retired in the early

Bessie and W. T. Coyne wintering in Florida, 1954

1950s—comfortable in a brick house, able to give his grandchildren savings bonds, free to take three-month vacations to Florida, where he spent the days at dog and horse races, with his wife always beside him in flowered dresses and a wad of bills forever bulging like frill from his pocket, caught in the teeth of his money clip. He once sent me a postcard with oranges in a truck on the front. It showed how oranges were picked—by the ton—and bore the caption, "Mining Florida Gold." There was a single line on the back. *Hope you are getting that score up at the bowling alley.*

ৰ৯৯

My father had been taking steps for some years to have a life like
W. T.'s.

Before he returned to Firestone from the war, T. W. bartered with
the company. He told Firestone he wouldn't return as an hourly
worker anymore. He wanted to be a supervisor, and he didn't want
to join a union—what I always remember him calling *an outside or-
ganization.*

In the 1930s, when he cured tires, he had been a member of the
United Rubber Workers, Local 7, clock card #9786. The union was
founded in the Portage Hotel of Akron just one year before T. W.
Coyne joined the company. I'm sure my father remembered the long
strike of ten thousand Firestone workers in 1937 just before the Wag-
ner Act was declared constitutional, and he wanted no more part of
that. Sit-down strikes must have frightened him. They stopped a
plant—brought the machines in my dad's beloved Xylos to a halt.
There was always the danger of beatings and threats and weapons
and bombings. It wasn't the kind of atmosphere my father thrived
in. He must have been afraid all the time the strike went on.

Now, in the 1940s, the son of a twenty-year man—a *comptroller,*
after all—now a smart young man with a letter from the company in
his hand asking him to come home from war, T. W. Coyne wanted to
be a *manager.* Not just a *Soldier* of Production, but at least a lieu-
tenant. He might not be able to rise in the ranks quite the way his father had, but one thing he knew. He didn't want a clock card number after his name anymore. He wanted a *title.*

Firestone gave him exactly what he wanted. In 1944 he came
back to Akron as a supervisor in the Xylos plant.

By 1950 he was a foreman, and on his way up. He bought a money clip, just like his father's, and kept it stuffed with bills for the rest
of his life.

T. W. Coyne, Xylos supervisor, to the right of man holding drink

⧬⧬⧬

In the 1980s, long after W. T. died, and long after I had moved away from Firestone Park, an amazing thing occurred on a road a little east of our house and a little south of the house where my grandpa lived. A house began to collapse in front of people's eyes. Each day it seemed to sink a little farther out of view. It slowly withdrew from the world, showing less and less of itself—less wall, less window, *more* roof—until it finally disappeared into an abandoned mine shaft.

This is how I first learned that there had once been coal in Akron. I wondered what W. T. would have thought had he known that the town he came to in order to *escape* coal had a warren of old mine shafts buried beneath it.

A series of connected basins of bituminous coal, four- to six-feet thick, began as far north as Cuyahoga Falls and formed all across the southern townships of Summit County. Some of the richest pockets, the same #1 coal mined in Mahoning County, were in Firestone Park, in my grandpa's own backyard. Berea sandstone, then Cuyahoga shale, then Carboniferous Conglomerate, and then coal—that's the simple geology of the bedrock close to my grandpa's house. If you see the conglomerate rock on the surface, a coarse yellowish sandstone—as you do in northern townships of Summit County, where I live now—you will never find coal, because coal always lies above it. Near the house where my grandpa lived, you won't see exposed conglomerate rock.

Coal was mined on both sides of Arlington Street, from Wilbeth to a little south of Waterloo Road, after it was found on Alexander Brewster's farm in 1848. The post office for the Brewster Coal Company was about where Arlington Plaza is today. Alexander Brewster built a five-mile railroad from his mines to the Ohio Canal—running the track along the lower end of Grant Street, under the Nypano rails near Thornton, and beside Wolf Run to the Lower Basin of the canal, a quarter mile south of Exchange Street. His father, Stephen, had traveled in 1812 to Akron from his former home in New York in an ox cart and built a log cabin in the woods he bought.

That land—Brewster Woods—was the eventual site of Roswell Kent Junior High, where I went to school, and of Suicide Hill, the slope kids ran down in the summer and sledded down when the last school bell rang in winter. My grandfather lived practically across the street from one of the richest reserves of coal in this part of the state.

He had no interest in Pennsylvania coal, and he never spoke

about the Brewster mines. Maybe he really never knew about them, or about the seven hundred men employed in the coal mines of Summit County in 1870. Or maybe he did, and just didn't care. I could see him grimace every time my father told the old stories of Pennsylvania coal to me. Grandpa would light a cigarette, leave the room, turn on his television—*anything* to keep from listening to tales of coal, or joining in.

Coal had been my grandpa's life for over thirty years. His family's *whole* life before him. You can't forget something that long and deep, can you? It would be impossible, I think, even if you tried.

It may have been my grandfather's attempt to forget the mines that caused his *own* collapse.

W. T. admitted no connection between the mines and the rubber plants, and yet those connections were so real and so profound that he must have felt them even as his silence denied that they were there. There was a restlessness about my grandpa that suggested something was after him, that he would *never* get the distance he wanted between those coal seams and the mahogany furniture of a comptroller's office. He always seemed nervous to me—short-tempered—like a man who had boarded the wrong train.

He made me nervous too.

W. T. would pace back and forth from the kitchen to the living room of his house, his hands behind him, the fingers of one hand fluttering like wings, the fingers of the other clenched so tight that his knuckles turned white. After he died, I noticed for the first time that he had worn a slick path between those rooms. Back and forth in his slippers he went, looking for something that had no form or name.

Sometimes I admired his restlessness, especially in the last years of his life. When he was in the hospital fifteen years before his death, he decided it was not the place for him. He didn't want to die then, and he certainly didn't want to die *there.* So W. T. crawled out a window in his hospital gown, coiled down a fire escape, and hailed a taxi home.

I remember thinking it *was* a horrible place, that hospital room. I hated to visit my grandpa there, and I was proud of him for running away. During a long hospital stay of my own many years later, I would dream about him. He stood outside my window, crooking his finger at me, like a hook, his white gown and white hair furious in the wind.

But things got a lot worse after his heroic exit. He grew angrier and angrier with his wife when Bessie forgot things, especially when she salted her famous thick brown gravy so heavily that you couldn't even swallow it, and it ruined the meat and potatoes underneath. That was the Sunday afternoon when he told T. W. to get Bessie out of his house. We packed up Grandma and took her to a nursing home.

After Bessie left the Reed Avenue house, W. T. argued with my mother (who *never* argued) and with my father, and finally told them not to come around anymore. We hired a woman to make dinner for Grandpa, Mother drove up and stripped the beds and ran the vacuum on Saturday mornings (not saying a word to W. T., nor he to her), and I stopped by after school every day to mix his medicines and make sure he took his pills. I placed them by his chair and disappeared without a word, without ever hearing another story that W. T. Coyne had to tell.

My father didn't know then, as no one did, that in twenty years his wife, Annabelle, would make the same gravy that his mother had. He didn't know that he, too, would have the power to decide how his wife would spend her final years.

Grandpa sent his wife away, then left us all. But he had started to take his leave years before his wife's memory stalled and his own health began to fail. He left us for Nebraska, for Pottstown, for Des Moines, for Florida orange groves and fast horses running circles on a track. He left Bessie because she slowed him down. No one knew what Alzheimer's was then, but he knew he'd *lose* if he placed a bet on *her*.

Maybe he was looking for something, and that's why he stayed on the move. Maybe he was just running, or trying to hide. Maybe this was all about survival—the only way he knew to keep alive. Maybe he just could never bear the world when it got too hard. Maybe things were just not adding up anymore, and so they made no sense to a man like him. A man of order and numbers and infinite precision.

Maybe one night he had dreamed that someone rolled a piece of Pennsylvania coal all the way down the Appalachian strain toward Ohio, and that it picked up steam on the alleyway, even picked up pieces of Akron coal, grew bigger and bigger, got faster and faster, until it rolled right over him in his fine dark suit, and he disappeared into the rock, and no one came to look for him.

Maybe that's why I always saw a light on in his bedroom window after Bessie left, when I'd drive by his house at night with my girl-friends on our way to Lujan's Burger Boy.

Maybe that's why he kept the doors and windows closed and stopped sitting in the metal chair on his porch.

Maybe that explains why the last thing he touched was Lord Elgin in the pocket of his pants. Not Bessie anymore, and certainly not us.

CHAPTER 6

❧❧❧

They both talked about some of the same things, T. W. and W. T. Like poodles and Cadillacs. Both subjects came up all the time, but Grandpa *owned* those things, and we never did. That was another difference between my father and his dad.

Part of the reason we never had poodles and Cadillacs was that Dad never got the kind of pay my grandpa did. But it was more than that, because Mom and Dad were great savers and probably could have found a way to buy a fancy dog and a really fancy car later in their marriage. But Dad seemed to sense that a white curly dog with jewelry around its neck didn't belong in a rubber town anymore than it had near the mines. It would be an affront to your neighbor to walk a poodle down your block. A white poodle means you have a lot of leisure on your hands, and very little dirt.

And a big white Cadillac? Steering something like that down your driveway to buy a loaf of bread on Aster Avenue? Maybe if we had lived on the north side of Firestone Boulevard, in the Moore Reserve, where Firestone's executives had their homes, but not on Evergreen Avenue at the top of the hill. Not in a house without a rec room in the basement or a fish pond in the back yard. Not on a street where the houses were so close that you trimmed one side of a hedge and your neighbor trimmed the other.

That doesn't mean he didn't *want* the dog and the car sometimes. He did. "Going to trade up!" my dad would always say when it was time for the Tom Coynes to buy a new car. But unlike our neighbor and my grandpa, who really *did* purchase Cadillacs at Dave Towell's, it was always a Plymouth or Dodge, later a small Chrysler, that ended up in our garage.

Something always kept Mr. Coyne from moving up too far.

❦❦❦

Our neighbor lady had them both—a poodle and a long white Cadillac. My dad loved her and hated her, and that's probably how he felt about his father too. I came to understand a lot about my father and his dad by watching Tom Coyne stew over that wealthy widow who lived across the street from us.

When I was growing up, my dad would glance starry-eyed out his living-room window in the morning as our neighbor in her white chenille bathrobe lifted her garage door (so all the neighbors could see the gleaming chrome of her Cadillac, I'm pretty sure), and then walked her poodle down the street. By late afternoon he was ready to kill her with his bare hands. He may have felt the same ambivalence about his dad, but he had to keep quiet about *him.* He could *say* something about the widow lady.

Our neighbor walked with a mysterious limp, and was the smallest woman I'd ever seen. She was alive *because* she was small.

She had been in a terrible car accident in the 1950s and lost her husband. Well, not exactly *lost* him. She sort of killed him. She was driving their Cadillac out West while her husband read an Oklahoma map, and she rammed into the back of a truck. A second truck hit her Cadillac from behind.

Her husband was killed instantly. He was a huge man, thick and fleshy, and he didn't have a chance. There was just too much of him to miss. She was in the hospital for months, but eventually recovered. When the trucks pressed her vehicle flat, she had slid under the wheel—all ninety pounds of her.

She had rouged cheeks and penciled eyebrows, hats with wide

brims, like giant sunflowers, and, of course, the little white poodle—which also survived the crash. The dog seemed to remember the accident better than the neighbor lady (who never spoke of it in all the years I knew her). It refused to hop obediently into a car ever again and just sat in the driveway and whined when our neighbor opened the door to the passenger side and tried to coax it in. She would have to pick the dog up, toss it in, and slam the door—fast—because it would start to growl and snap at her the instant it felt the leather of the seat scrape its belly.

I knew there was something different about the woman across the street, and I knew it had something to do with that poodle. To me she was the most elegant woman on earth—after Idabelle Firestone, of course. No one else on our street was having tea in the middle of the afternoon. But *she* was. And *I* sometimes joined her.

"Teatime!" she'd say on the phone, and across the street I'd go.

She served a little crusty dab of this or that. It always tasted old, like icebox air. But it appeared on English porcelain (*Staffordshire,* she told me) with gold edges—not chalky plates like my mother's beige and green wedding china from Japan. While we ate, she played records on an old Victrola. Always in the background were singers with rich, wavy voices warbling away in a language as beautiful and indecipherable to me as birdsong.

She dressed in white blouses and black slacks, but she always had pinned to her collar a piece of jewelry with pretty stones. She collected Royal Doulton figurines, and let me hold them, her own hands carefully cupped underneath mine. Nearly every one was a statue of a beautiful woman with a cat or a dog or an umbrella glued to her side.

"There's a way to hold beautiful things," she told me. A way to do everything, and she proceeded to show me what it was.

She talked about *her* bankers at Firestone Bank, and *her* ministers at *her* church who were taking *her* to Hawaii (and, I'm sure she thought, to *heaven* too). I was sure she owned half of Akron. The half that Harvey didn't.

She would sometimes invite me to the rose garden behind her house. She would always wear soft leather gloves to work in, the kind my mother and I only wore to church. She talked about Europe and great singers, her saint of a husband (she spoke of him always in the present tense, ignoring his death more persistently with each passing year), and her *new* Cadillac from Dave Towell's that replaced the one she wrecked and *never* talked about. As far as I could tell, her friends (except for me, of course) were all attorneys and physicians, and she referred to them as "Dr. This" and "Mr. That." She told me about fancy restaurants where she ate French cheese and leg of lamb and escargot, and about the cleaning woman she had fired earlier in the day because *she just wouldn't do.*

Her house was no more than a small cottage, really, but the poodle and the Cadillac, the figurines and roses, the long stream of cleaning women made it seem like a picture I'd seen in my *World Book Encyclopedia* of an English manor in the countryside.

She would cut a single rose before I left and place it in my hands, and I would hurry home to follow her directions for keeping it alive. To this day, if a rose I cut from my own garden wilts too fast, I smell her dry breath in the room.

At night, my dad glared at our neighbor from the same living-room window he had looked through with such longing in the morning. He watched her sneak across the street to our sidewalk, dragging the poodle and a garbage bag behind her, and quickly head for the trash can we'd just put out on our devil's strip—Akron's curious name for the swatch of grass between the sidewalk and the street. While the dog peed on our aluminum container, our neighbor lifted the lid and plopped in the chicken bones and tea bags from the afternoon party the two of us had enjoyed. I felt responsible somehow, and wondered if my father blamed me too.

"Tossing garbage in our can again, Annabelle!" my dad would yell to my mother as he moved toward the front door, not really caring if his wife heard, or even if she was in the room. "Thinks she owns the block!"

I knew he'd never *really* open the door and yell at our neighbor, even though I saw his hand clenched on the doorknob as if his fingers had melted into bronze and he couldn't get free. He'd settle down by morning and be peeking through the curtain at that cute little poodle dog again. And I'd be sitting right beside him, hoping that when our neighbor went inside she'd call me up and ask me if I'd come for tea.

≈≈≈

I never knew when the subject of poodles would arise. The neighbor and her dog often brought it on, but not always. It was certain, though, that Dad would have something important to say about poodles at the Firestone Christmas party for kids, the high point of the year for children of Firestone employees.

The Christmas show was held in the clubhouse auditorium (which doubled as the gym), but when I was young I thought that space was *only* for the Christmas show. Tinsel braids festooned the huge room, and there was silver everywhere. I loved everything about the Firestone Christmas party—the magnificent tree, Santa Claus himself (there was no doubt in my mind that Firestone's Santa was the real one, and all the others fake), clowns with tiny hats and painted grins. Sometimes, the clowns reminded me of my aunts, who used red lipstick to make their upper lips seem bigger than they really were.

Author with Santa Claus

The animal acts were best. Over the years we fell in love with un-countable monkeys, parrots, horses, and dogs. Dogs were our favorite. We *always* expected at least one dog, no matter what other animals performed.

About every other year a white poodle disappeared into the ceiling of the stage. It bounced off a trampoline, sailed into the air, and just never came down. A little later it ran in from the side of the stage and surprised newcomers. My dad was hardly a newcomer, so *surprise* wasn't exactly the emotion he registered. *Amazement* or *admiration* might be a better word to describe Tom Coyne's response to the little poodle dog when it vanished in the air. He never grew tired of the trick, that much I know.

"See that!" Tom Coyne nudged me. "No animal on God's green earth is smarter than a poodle!" He talked as if intelligence was a factor in what we'd just seen the dog do (or what was done to the dog).

Every time my dad saw a poodle—on the street, yapping in the back seat of a car, pressed like a clutch purse under some woman's meaty arm in a grocery store—he said something about poodles being the smartest animal alive. His favorite line—the clincher—was, "That's why they use them in the circus."

At the company Christmas party, my father's passion for poodles was so intense that he sounded like the singers on my neighbor's records when he talked about them. His enthusiasm may have had something to do with his company obviously liking poodles too. Tom Coyne liked it when *his* policies, and *Firestone* policies, were the same.

෨෧ෑ

Although Tom Coyne was *on his way up* in the 1950s, just the way his father had been thirty years before, I think his memory was better than W. T.'s, and it kept him from getting so puffed up—so light and fragile—that a strong wind might carry him away.

Those lumps of coal that lined his pockets in the early years *always* weighed him down, even when he traded them for his *own* pocket watch from Firestone. I guess I always saw coal in his pockets, even when I knew the watch was there. Maybe because coal meant stories—memories of the place and people who brought him here, who brought us all here—and the stories *never* disappeared.

I saw coal when he told about the mountains and Pennsylvania, when he refused to buy a poodle dog (before the parakeets, my parents always had yappy mixed breeds like Rusty, who was a little Pekingese and a whole lot something else), when he insisted on cutting the grass for neighbors who were sick—wheeling his lawnmower as quietly as he could into their yards before he pulled the cord and made the engine roar so loudly that every dog and cat on the street began to bark and snarl, and the birds darted from bushes and trees for the power lines in our backyards.

When I look at my dad's first company picture, I like to think it's coal that makes his pocket bulge. I pretend there wasn't a single day that he forgot to carry it, and that it helped my dad when life turned mean and cruel.

When he died, I gave my father's rings and razors to the men in our family. I kept his Firestone pins, his medals from the war, his company watch.

But what I wanted more than anything was to find those lumps of coal. I looked in every drawer the day I chose my father's funeral clothes. The coal wasn't there.

When I cleaned his house, getting ready for the sale, my hands shook each time I pressed a thumb to an unopened box. I stood on ladders so I could peer into corners of dark closet shelves.

I thought the lumps might be in his safety deposit box, so I hurried to my father's bank when I found the key. There was nothing. Only his favorite coins (Tom Coyne loved coins), a tiny silver tray, the round metal frames from the first glasses he ever wore.

I never found the coal. I know I never will.

But sometimes I dream about it. I dream of being a little girl again and reaching into my father's pocket for the coal, and for the stories he would recite when I placed it in his hand. I dream of sitting under our apple tree together, listening to my dad, turning the coal slowly while he would read each surface and tell me what it said. I dream of stealing the coal from him and storing the lumps in a canning jar in our fruit cellar, like dark blue plums, climbing in a small basement window at night to look at them because the house no longer belongs to us and the cellar is not our own.

But then I wake and know I can't take the coal or keep it safe. It is my father's, it's not mine. Without him the stories disappear and the coal is just a piece of rock.

I cannot make sense of skeletons or trilobites pressed into the coal without my dad. It's my father's breath that always brought stone alive, and now his memory traveling on the wind is all that's left to give the fossils life.

When It Came to Safety . . .

Akron journalists have recently uncovered new details about the 1950 Dedication. If my father had known then what journalists know now, I wonder if he would have stayed with the company. Maybe he would have walked straight up Main Street and found another job, but probably nothing would have changed. He would have kept on whistling the Firestone Jingle. Trouble had to get closer to my father's skin before he'd stop hearing that tune in his head.

A small deception had been at work the afternoon in 1950 when Harvey's five sons removed the veil from the bronze shoulders of their famous father. James Earle Fraser, the sculptor of Harvey Firestone who had also created statues of Theodore Roosevelt and General George S. Patton, had not finished Harvey. But the Firestone Tire & Rubber Company refused to postpone the Dedication, so nervous planners arranged to have Fraser's full-size plaster model painted bronze and shipped to Firestone Park from the Gorham Foundry in Rhode Island. All the pictures of Harvey that day with his sons looking up at him are pictures of a statue as flimsy as a piñata.

About a month later, James Earle Fraser completed the bronze, and in the middle of the night the fake statue was hauled away and hidden behind one of Firestone's plants, where it would later be destroyed. All but Harvey's head, that is. The Firestone project director could not summon the courage to take a sledgehammer to the head of the company founder, so when it rolled onto the ground, detached from a body that now lay in pieces, he took it home, like a souvenir hunter near the guillotine. He kept it in his house until his wife couldn't stand it anymore, and then smashed it into pieces and set it out on the devil's strip on trash day. No one knew the whole story of the statue until David Giffels found it out and wrote a column in the Beacon Journal *just a few years ago.*

Even though the plaster statue remained a secret for over forty years, there were always signs that things in Firestone Park were not as solid as they seemed. Those of us who lived there could have read them, but we did-n't. We lived in Harvey's town, the place of his own making, but we came to think of it as our own. It never was. It was as if the Firestone family had flown in scenery for a movie about a perfect kingdom—streets and build-ings, schools and churches. Everything. We were no more than the loyal subjects who brought it all to life, people in a play whose lines came from a script.

CHAPTER 7

I grew up hearing my father belt out safety slogans in the shower. He couldn't carry a tune—but he could memorize Firestone dogma without any trouble at all. I can still hear those slogans spilling out into the hall, pouring right into my bedroom. "Safety for Sure Is the Accident Cure!" "Safety Is Free, Try It and See!" "Let's Not Coast— Keep Safety Foremost!"

I sang the slogans too, with the same inflection I heard in my father's voice.

Xylos was the sponsor of an annual safety contest for all the plants, maybe because Xylos was the most dangerous plant of all and it made sense for it to lead the campaign. My father helped with the contest for a long time.

He'd draw names of clock employees on each shift and then give them a chance to win a silver dollar if they could quote the new safety slogan. Sometimes I'd see pictures of winners in the *Non-Skid*, Firestone's in-house newsletter. I liked the rhymes, but I really had no idea how important safety was in an industry like rubber in those years, or in a place like Xylos. My father liked jingles too, but unlike me, he knew the danger that was always at his back.

I wonder now when he first sensed that all the jingles, the safety slogans—even the steel plates he wore in his shoes—wouldn't protect him from the real dangers of his job.

Xylos isn't standing anymore. Where Xylos used to be there's only a parking lot. The Akron police use it sometimes for training exercises. It feels funny to drive down Emerling Avenue and see only asphalt and orange cones where a five-story building—200,000 square feet of building—used to stand.

When I was growing up, trucks with loads of bald and weary tires wobbled and snorted every day down the streets of Akron toward Xylos. A good friend recently removed about fifty old tires from his father's backyard, getting the house ready to sell after his dad died. I realized how much things had changed when he stopped by on his way to dispose of the tires and said that he was going to have to *pay* someone five dollars apiece to take the things off his hands.

That hard spot of asphalt was a busy place when Xylos, and my dad, were in their prime, when the old tires that trucks and trains unloaded there still had value. For thirty-seven years Xylos was what my dad breathed right after the fumes of his morning coffee swirled up his nose.

Reclaim was the dirtiest job at the factory. Every step of the process involved filth. Old tires were received in the shipping yard, sorted into piles, cut into chunks. Then the metal was sifted out and the tire scrap was mixed with solutions of carbon black, solvents like sodium hydroxide and Xylene (thus, *Xylos*), and other chemicals that helped process old rubber so that it could be used again.

The reclaimed rubber was rolled into thin sheets only an inch thick, and then shipped to a manufacturing room to become new products—Rub-R-Road and Rub-R-Trac paving materials, floor mats, sidewalls. Some of the parks in the city had recreational surfaces that began on the wheels of Cadillacs and were born again in the Xylos plant. Ours might have, in Firestone Park, but I'm not sure of that. I may have skinned my knees on flakes of rubber ground up from the tires my dad shredded in his plant.

Weary Akron tires being hauled to a reclaim plant
(*Photo by Jim Root. Courtesy of the* Akron Beacon Journal)

Carbon black (which my dad always called *lampblack*) was the culprit that covered him with soot at the end of a day. Those little fluffy particles that aided in smoothing reclaim material and improving its quality were produced out of town and then shipped to Akron in tank cars. My dad sometimes laughed about having to dust his office furniture with a piece of cheesecloth in the morning, but I always felt it made him feel important too. It let us know that Tom Coyne *had* a desk, a filing cabinet, a swivel chair.

But he didn't laugh when he came home every afternoon caked

Old tires ready for reclaim, Xylos, 1934 (Courtesy of Bridgestone/Firestone, Inc.)

in carbon black. " 'EL-lope!" I'd hear Dad yell when he opened the back door. He'd let out a great sigh and then walk toward the nearby laundry chute. It was almost as if the architect knew my dad would one day own this house and need to shed the filth of Xylos before he stepped into his Tudor dream. Next, there was the sound of his struggle with dirty clothes ("E-Gads!")—with zippers, buttons, belts—as he stripped down to his boxer shorts. Then, the final whoosh of fabric sliding down that metal chute. Sometimes a seam or buttonhole would catch on a sharp piece of metal and Dad would jab the cloth with a broom handle to coax it loose. I'd hear him straining in his wild, forlorn way. The sound was always deep and sad, like some great bird honking across the sky. It would have been easier to have walked the clothes down the basement stairs to the laundry basket, but we had a *chute* in our fancy house, and my father was going to use it, *by gum.*

One of my strongest memories, literally burned into my senses, is the odor of bleach drifting up our cellar steps. My mother had a huge silver tub that she used just for my dad's shirts and socks and handkerchiefs. She'd massage Dad's clothes with Clorox in her Platex Living Gloves. To this day the odor of bleach brings tears to my eyes. I can hardly stand it.

In the Firestone complex Xylos was the most *dangerous* plant, as well as the dirtiest. It must have been a war zone inside that five-story brick building. There were tanks of caustic chemicals, a hog mill with huge rotating steel rolls, piles of tires stacked high and heavy everywhere, giant mechanical scissors that cut the chunks of rubber down. A digester rose three stories straight through the center of the building and belched sour air into south Akron twenty-four hours a day. It was the smell of Xylos that drove executives west to their fine homes on the lee side of the factories.

Throughout the 1950s, first as a foreman, and then as manager of materials preparation at Xylos, Tom Coyne was praised for keeping his men safe. In one photograph from 1953, my then-thin father, sporting one of his wide and wild print ties, proudly accepts a safety award from a Firestone executive. He was forty-seven years old when that picture was taken, younger than I am now. He still looks vigorous and healthy. His hair is brown and wavy (with a little help from Vitalis) and his smile is enormous, like a circus clown's.

My dad's obsession with safety didn't stop when he left the

T. W. Coyne, right, accepting a safety award for Xylos, 1953

plant. He brought it home with him. He couldn't help it, I know that now, but at the time he made us all a little crazy. When I place a magnifying glass on top of the photograph of my father receiving the safety award, I see under it a picture of myself in the 1950s— a photograph of the safest girl in town. I'm not really there, of course, but I always wanted to tell my side of the story, so maybe that's why I see this awkward child standing there, waiting for her turn. My father was proud of being safe, but the girl in that picture was not.

Try to imagine what *I* can. Try to hear the words that were never spoken by a girl in a photo that doesn't exist.

෨෨෨

Most people don't worry all that much about a thing like shoes, but we do in our house. A lot. I don't mean the usual worries—the style of the new shoes you buy for school each fall, the size and shape of the heel on your silver tap shoes every year (taller heels mean you're old enough to have a period, so my heels are flat), the special shoes you buy for Easter or First Communion.

We worry in our family about having our feet cut off. And what we can do to prevent it.

Dad shows me articles about safety shoes in Non-Skids. *That's how my worry first began. There's a story in almost every issue about someone whose toes or feet have been saved because they wore safety shoes to work, with a picture of people acting out what really happened. I've read stories of one-ton hoist lifts rolling onto feet, tire molds crashing through the air right toward someone's ankle, huge buckets dropping directly onto someone's ten little piggies. The stories are written by the people who wore the shoes and have toes left to prove it.*

There are safety cartoons in the Non-Skids *too. Puzzles, really. One cartoon was labeled "How Many Safety Faults Can You Find in This Picture?" There was a ladder poking through a window because the person carrying it wasn't looking ahead of him, seeping cans of oil, bare bulbs, slick rags on a set of steps, a sign that said, "Spit Anywhere You Like." I stared at the mess on the page and got so worried that I ran upstairs and cleaned my room.*

I have to wear safety shoes to make my dad happy, and to remove some of the daily terror I have about losing my feet. I wrote a story called "My Fear of Defeat" for school a couple years ago and it had a double meaning, but I never told my dad that. I have enough trouble with my feet without worrying about losing them, believe me, and I think about them all the time as it is.

My dad actually was classified as "limited service" in the army because of fallen arches. I inherited those very feet, and by the time I was six years old was going to a foot specialist. I still have to do exercises with marbles—picking them up by curling my toes around them. It hurts, and the marbles are always cold. I'm not sure why marbles are cold, but they are. And I have to wear special shoes with arch supports—orthopedic shoes, they're called—that I buy at a place where the clerks all look like nurses.

My regular shoes are ugly, heavy, and different from other little girls' shoes to begin with, but when Dad shoves steel tips in the toes, they're even worse.

I feel like the bottom-heavy bobos our parakeets all love to knock around, or those clowns you can inflate and punch that are weighted down with sand. My little bird legs are attached to cartoon feet, and I hurry to school each morning so I can push my shoes under my desk out of everyone's view—especially my own.

☙ ❧

My father's gift of flat arches wasn't enough. He also gave me his nearsightedness. My mother never has trouble with her feet, except for occasional corns on her little toes, and her vision is perfect. I'm convinced that parents slip their children bad genes like Old Maid cards. Life is going just great until you turn that card over and see an ugly old woman with thick glasses and safety shoes. And you realize it's you.

One of the most terrifying experiences of my life was having my eyes examined two years ago. I knew I would fail. I hadn't ever failed a test before, and I didn't like the idea at all. But the PTA purchased eye-testing equipment when I was in fourth grade and conducted hun-

dreds of eye exams. I wanted perfect attendance for the year, so I couldn't pretend to be sick and stay home. Besides, there were make-up days for the test if you happened to miss it.

I remember seeing the huge L and T at the top of a chart perched on the chalk holder of the blackboard, but I couldn't read much below that. A parent volunteer held a card over each eye, and two other mothers covered rows of letters on the chart, working their way down to specks of black the size of fleas. The chart was about twenty feet away, but it may as well have been on a different planet. The PTA volunteers were so surprised at how poorly I did that they traded the letter chart for one with bunnies.

"Are the bunny's ears up or down?" they asked.

I shrugged my little shoulders.

"Right or left?"

I couldn't even see the stupid bunny, let alone his ears, but those well-meaning moms persisted. I guess they brought in the bunny chart because they thought I might be really slow and didn't know how to read.

Just a few fourth graders had vision below 20/30, but I was one of them. I didn't pass and had to be retested by a nurse. That, of course, didn't go any better for me than the PTA experience. So, the dreaded event finally occurred. A letter was sent home.

And that led to my first pair of glasses—swooped-wing things in blue aluminum frames with rhinestones clear across the top. I knew they were a little fancy for everyday, but I thought that as long as I had to wear them I may as well get ones that were my favorite color, and had some sparkle to them. Just like stars.

The whole effect was ruined by the safety glass my father insisted on. He showed me some of the Wise Owl Club testimonies from his Non-Skids to try to convince me this was a good idea, just as he had *shown me the people with safety shoes. To be a member of the Wise Owl Club, you had to have just missed going blind because safety lenses had saved your sight. It didn't seem like a club you'd really want to belong to all that much. To me the Mickey Mouse Club was a lot more appealing, and I thought Annette Funicello was about the cutest girl in the whole world. Being a Mouseketeer and owning a club sweater were things I wanted a lot more than having my eyes knocked out of their sockets.*

About this time my father made me read more testimonials, ones about metal flying off chisels, clasps snapping, bits breaking off electric drills. If you could imagine it, it was flying through the air right toward someone's eyeballs. My dad told me the air inside Firestone was as full of flak as London skies during the Blitz.

Dad thought the lenses were a good deal. My eyes would be protected from any meteorites that might fall in Akron, and the company would pay five dollars for each pair of prescription lenses. It was like getting something for free, Dad said.

I think what finally convinced me more than anything to go ahead with the lenses was my fourth-grade teacher. She was an older woman, and she always carried a small clock around. Not a wristwatch or even a pocket watch like my grandpa's, but a clock *in a leather case—a real* clock *with exposed metal hands that you actually could feel, if you wanted to. She didn't* want *to, she* had *to. My teacher was almost legally blind, and in order to keep to the schedule of the school day, she had to touch the hands of the clock every few minutes to find out what time it was. We loved her and were very protective of her, but I think having her the year my eyes flunked was probably a very bad thing. I was sure I was going blind, just like my teacher. And I didn't want to carry a clock around the rest of my life, not even if I could get one with a rhinestone face.*

The safety lenses made my glasses at least twice as thick as anyone else's. There weren't many fourth graders wearing glasses to begin with. I was afraid to ask my dad why this amount of protection was necessary. It just didn't make sense to me. Still doesn't. Before the lenses, nothing except my eyelids protected my eyes from peril, but suddenly I needed something as thick as a windshield in front of me.

Don't get me wrong, I liked seeing the blackboard again, but I didn't like being laughed at. One boy started blowing a whistle at me on the playground right after I had the lenses installed.

"Look at the grouse!" he said, then blew away and pointed at me. And I thought to myself, Go ahead, Buster, throw something at my eyes, drop something on my foot! See what good it does you! *Later I wondered what kind of grouse wore safety glasses, or even what a grouse was.*

༄༅

I guess that what my dad really has done by his obsession with safety, since nothing ever targets my feet or my eyes, is keep me safe from boys a little longer, and that means sex. Boys are sort of repelled by the shoes and the glasses, to tell you the truth, though my girlfriends never seem to mind. Why would they? With those feet and my prescription for eyeglass lenses, I've reduced the competition in our town for boys by one.

Picture this. A typical Saturday afternoon working in the yard at my house. There's my dad cutting the hedges with his wide, wooden-handled trimmers, safety goggles strapped to his head, and safety toes in his shoes. Mother is sitting on the ground edging the lawn and pulling juicy dandelions, with a similar pair of goggles over her eyes. And there I am, in those steel shoes and bulletproof glasses, following right behind.

Safe as can be.

CHAPTER 8

☙☙☙

When it came to safety, and almost everything else, my dad listened to the company. Believed what it told him. *In Firestone We Trust* was the motto on *his* dollar bills.

Tom Coyne was *gum-dipped,* a term used in the rubber industry to describe managers who were absolutely loyal to the company and wore clean white shirts that smelled good in the morning. It doesn't sound like a very flattering term—the actual process of gum-dipping fabric made it uniform—but my dad was proud of what he was, and my mom and I were proud of him too.

My father believed that rubber would make all the world's troubles bounce away from him, just the way that nylon cord dipped in rubber *(gum-dipped)* and then pressed into the tread let tires roll more buoyantly down the road. Flexible, resilient, cool.

There was *an understanding* at Firestone—at least my dad used to say it this way—that if you were loyal to the company and its values (*gum-dipped,* in other words), you would have a job for life. He said the words *for life* all the time, like it was a promise. Or a sentence.

So Tom Coyne did what the company told him for a long, long time. For decades. When Firestone offered incentives in the *Non-Skid* to men who *used their brain,* my father enrolled in courses the Firestone Tire & Rubber Company sponsored for its employees. *If you use your brain,* early *Non-Skid*s promised, you could be promoted and *get the big pay.*

My dad was *always* taking night courses, though they never added up to a college degree, or even a certificate. They didn't add up to anything. I remember him practicing speeches on the heavy metal Wollensak reel-to-reel tape recorder he bought just for his public speaking class. Recording those speeches. Playing them back. Recording them again.

He always told me success came from adopting a *positive, forceful approach* and building a good vocabulary. Consequently, he developed a great stentorian voice and a frantic passion for new words that eventually even his crossword puzzle dictionary couldn't satisfy. So one Christmas Mr. Webster, unabridged, paid a visit to our house, marched into our living room and stood at attention on my dad's coffee table, waiting to serve Mr. Coyne.

My father brought his Firestone education home with him, the same way he brought those reinforced toes and safety lenses.

While he practiced his speeches in the living room, he asked my mother and me to heckle him sometimes, the way he said men did in class. After just a few seconds of clapping our hands and whistling and pointing at him and laughing, we could tell it made him nervous, so we stopped. My mother told me Dad got enough criticism without us giving him more. She said that even before the criticism at work began to come in my dad's direction hard and fast.

He would sit on his sofa Saturday and Sunday evenings, reading books by Dale Carnegie—*How to Win Friends and Influence People, How to Stop Worrying and Start Living*—and take pages and pages of notes, trying to get ready for speech class. His collection of Dale Carnegie books gradually squeezed out his beloved Zane Grey.

The only interruption he would allow was *Maverick* on Sunday nights. He loved James Garner—that tall dark gamblin' man. I think a part of my father—not the part seated on the sofa doing his homework for Firestone, but the other part that was somewhere else and despised the Wollensak—identified with Bret Maverick, so suave, but quick with his fists and gun when he needed to be.

On the weekend he dressed like Maverick might have if he'd lived in the middle of the twentieth century and worked for Firestone. Maverick liked ruffled shirts, thin cigars, black ribbon ties around his neck. On Saturday mornings, my dad pushed his hangers forward to get to the flowered shirts in the back of his closet—bright nylon blousy things that hung over his belt and had big pockets on the sides. He bought them on our Florida vacations. If there were errands to run, he'd add a cherry red driving hat to his ensemble.

Dad whistled the Firestone jingle on weekdays, the Maverick theme song on weekends. He had a mighty whistle that attracted every cardinal in the neighborhood. Maybe the birds liked the bright red hat he wore, and mistook him for one of their own when they spotted the color and the bill that jutted out. He tossed peanuts to them in the driveway, then did a cardinal imitation that was so convincing that a swarm of bright red birds invariably gathered at the feeding spot, like pools of swirling blood.

I think my dad also liked the Maverick theme song because it had the word "Annabelle" in it.

"It's the only song with your mother's name!" he'd say to me. He'd sing it trimming the hedges outside or driving in the car on errands, especially if my mom was his passenger. *Riverboat ring your bell! / Fare-thee-well ANNABELLE! / Luck is the lady that he loves the best!*

That song was the closest my father ever came to flirting with my mom, and it never failed to annoy her.

The Firestone jingle was the *real* song in my father's life, of course. Rubber, he told me, was the solid thing *our* family was built upon, and I believed him. Like my dad, I also believed that Firestone was for life, and I never really questioned it. It was as permanent and present as the statue at the entrance to our neighborhood, as strong as those gum-dipped tires we rode on.

But one day soon we'd both find out that we were wrong.

౨౪౨

It was important for Tom Coyne to pass his Firestone education onto his daughter. He taught me everything he knew about rubber.

Dad took me to the Firestone service store whenever he bought new tires and showed me how to spot *top quality*. To this day a car's tires are the first thing I see when I walk onto a lot, no matter how brightly the body gleams.

He walked me to the gas station on Aster Avenue—Leffler's— and helped me inflate my bike tires when I was six years old. At sweet sixteen, before my father let me on the road to drive with a temporary license (and certainly before he'd let me kiss a boy), he taught me how to change a flat.

I could read a pressure gauge as easily as a book. I knew early on that heat caused air to expand, so pressure had to be read when the tire was cold, not hot. I carried a six-inch ruler in the waist of my pants so I could stick it in the tread of my bike tires and measure it, the way my father did.

I would help him line up the chains he wrapped around his tires for the winter. We'd lay them on the ground in front of our car and then drive slowly forward until we could hook them around the wheels. When studded tires came in during the 1970s, my father put them on all *four* tires—not the recommended two in the rear.

"Twice as safe," he'd say, completely unaware that studded tires would rip roads apart, and states would soon have to outlaw them.

Together my father and I would wash our car on Saturday after-

T. W. Coyne explaining the world to author

noons. My job was to scrub the whitewalls—which my father insisted on having. Managers always had whitewalls, he said. I scrubbed them with a special cleaner and if a streak wouldn't disappear, my father would kneel on the ground with a toothbrush and use what he called "elbow grease." Those whitewalls were worth the trouble, my dad said, though I had a hard time understanding why that strip of white mattered to him the way it did.

"The Coynes have whitewalls," my dad said. Period. W. T. had them, and so would his son. My father even insisted that his daughter have them on her Firestone bikes.

Dad didn't stop with *practical* lessons about rubber, either. In my home I learned the *history* of rubber too, at least the version that my father taught.

Tom Coyne brought home raw rubber and charts about How Rubber Is Made and How Our Lives Would Be Different Without Rubber Products. Not just *different,* he added. *Worse.* He showed me a pamphlet with a Liberian man on the front, dressed in a white short-sleeved shirt that set off the brilliance of his black arms. His head was shaved, not all slicked down to get the wave out the way black people in Akron wore their hair when I was young. I remember being amazed by the color of the man, and by his bare feet. He stood in the middle of a jungle and cut thin strips of bark off trees until latex as white as his shirt oozed into a small ceramic bowl. Inside the pamphlet were stories with titles like "The White Man Discovers Rubber."

My dad didn't know much about Firestone going into Liberia. I remember asking him about the country, because we never mentioned it at school, and he just said it was hot and far away, but that Negroes liked heat like that more than white people and he was glad Firestone had bought Liberia.

Recently I found a 1950 *Beacon* commemorative issue that talked about Harbel Landing, Liberia, the lease Firestone took on Liberian land in 1924, and the 12,000 Liberians that Firestone employed in 1927. I also located a picture in a *Non-Skid* from the late 1930s that showed plantation managers fishing for barracuda and red snapper in the Farmington River, Liberia, near Marshall, a chief shipping point for Firestone. A *Non-Skid* from 1940 announced that a mem-

Liberian tapper (Courtesy of Bridgestone/Firestone, Inc.)

ber of Firestone's legal department had just visited Liberia and landed a 170-pound Tarpon that measured seven feet and was forty inches around the girth. "Liberia is a fisherman's paradise!" the lawyer
told Firestone reporters.

In Akron, black people worked for Firestone. But they didn't live
within the strict boundaries of Firestone Park. They lived closer to
the factories. There were no blacks in my elementary school. The
boundary lines for Akron's high schools had to be more generous,
so in tenth grade I suddenly found myself sitting beside blacks in
homeroom. But when we poured out the doors at the end of a day,
we walked in different directions. If you were black, you crossed
Archwood, generally at Grant Street, and headed north. Archwood
was the northern boundary line of the Park, an invisible fence sharper and more painful than razor wire.

Firestone never kept blacks out of its reclaim plant. There were probably as many blacks as whites who operated the machines at Xylos. Dad was keenly aware of the importance of setting boundaries between blacks and whites inside his plant, of having lines *he* would not cross. I always knew if Dad was talking about a white man or a black man because he called whites by their last names and blacks by their first. *Gamble* and *Miller* and *Mayberry* were white, but *Billy* and *Travis* and *Berthrem* were black. Sometimes at the Christmas parties a black man who worked for my dad would introduce us to his family.

The man would always call my dad "Mister Coyne." And then Mister Coyne would say, "Nice to meet your family, Walter!"

I'm not sure if my dad knew the real lesson he was teaching me when he talked about Harvey's empire and the way rubber was gathered in his West African colony. It was the image of a black man holding a knife that fascinated me most, even more than the rubber flowing down the fresh gashes in the bark.

CHAPTER 9

Elms branched over our streets, like cool arches, and at night lovers walked under them on curved roads lit by the glow of Harvey's streetlights.

Dad was certain we'd be safe here, in a place where privet hedges, not fences, divided one house from another.

Streets weren't laid out in conventional grids, the way they were in Goosetown. Harvey chose gentle curves. Our street, Evergreen, emptied into Crescent Drive, a climbing, curvy road that peaked high on a hill by my house and then slid down both sides to the Boulevard, where it formed two points, just like the ends of the crescent moon it was. Every day I rode my bike down that street, braked at the bottom of the hill (at South Firestone Boulevard), prayed no cars would slow me down (I had already forgotten that they could flatten me, the way they had my cousin Eddie), and then rolled the rest of the way into the park on my Firestone whitewalls.

It's astonishing to me that I never realized Crescent Drive was shaped like a first-quarter moon while I lived right on its edge all those years. The contours of that street may as well have been the contours of my body, I rode it so often, but I never felt its shape below me.

Only decades later did I happen to see an old map of my part of town and notice the crescent moon cutting up the hill, like a scythe. I saw other things on the map that day.

The streets that formed the boundaries of the park I played in

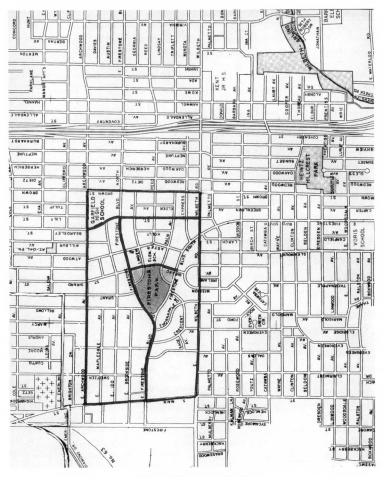

Map of Firestone Park

curved no more randomly than Crescent did. They followed a plan. They formed the script Firestone *F*, the famous *F* known all around the world. Harvey's landscape architect had cut the streets that way, gouged them out with Harvey's monogram. Firestone's signature was pressed into our roads, into our knees when we skinned them. It was pressed into our lives every minute that we lived in his town.

And most amazing of all, I saw that the park itself was part of the company plan. That shady place that seemed so soft and free and effortless in my girlhood—and in my memory all the years that followed—may as well have been a spot of green in a prison yard. It was cut in the perfect shape of the company shield, the crest that appeared on every Firestone ad and sign.

No one ever told me about these things. As far as I know, my father never knew—no one ever told *him,* either. It never crossed our minds back then that those curvy roads and that park were part of Harvey's plan to lure us in. All the time I thought I was dancing in the fairy rings of that enchanted place, I was really growing up inside company lines.

Mostly, *I* saw heaven.

❧❧

There *were* some signs that registered—that pricked my nerves and wouldn't bounce away—though I seldom stopped to add things up.

I was born *after* the war, but there were still reminders that this happy place had been touched by war, that it was not the refuge from all harm that my dad had wanted it to be. The war had come to the Park, and the Firestone Tire & Rubber Company had been largely responsible for bringing it there. In the 1940s the company built a bomb shelter out of heavy corrugated steel right on the corner of Firestone Boulevard and South Main, just down from my house and across the street from Harvey's statue. The company was convinced that rubber was so crucial to the mobilization of an army that Akron would be a prime target for the Axis. Everyone knows now that there never was a chance that a World War II plane could make it over this far (certainly not before the very end of the war, and then there wasn't enough fuel left to fill the new planes), but that never seemed to cross anyone's mind during the arrogant war years in Rubber Town.

The whole town was enormously inflated at this time, a little like its tires. The Rotary Club in Akron, like the Firestone plant, became convinced that the rubber companies were in grave danger and organized the Civil Defense Operation for the city. Akron's concerned Rotarians, a group of portly gentlemen who loved cigars, stood round the clock in two-hour shifts on the roof of the First National Bank Tower—Akron's version of a skyscraper—and plane-spotted with binoculars.

The company loved the shelter and for months sponsored public tours from noon to nine o'clock, and once a special lunch on plastic trays was served there to Firestone executives. People came to see all the equipment inside—a chemical toilet, sink, electric heater, oil cooking stove, lanterns, fire extinguishers, picks and shovels, stretchers and blankets. I never actually stepped inside the bomb shelter that Firestone constructed, but I knew about it, and it made me a little nervous thinking about gas and bombs dropping on my neighborhood, maybe in my own backyard.

During the years when Firestone held its circus on the corner of Wilbeth and Main, a four-hundred-pound Bengal tiger had once gotten loose and prowled the very street I lived on. It happened before I moved to the Park, but the older kids still talked about it all the time and tried to scare the younger kids with the story. Bombs never really dropped on Evergreen Avenue, and tigers never hunted when I lived there, but my imagination brought it all to life.

Nothing ever *really* happened. Even the shelter became boring.

It was converted to a scientific winter storage space for fresh vegetables. Bomb-proof cabbages, potatoes, carrots, beets, turnips, parsnips, and even rutabagas lived there now and received regular blasts from a machine that shot ultraviolet rays at spores and mold. Thirty tons of fresh vegetables were stored in the summer and fall and then served in the Firestone cafeteria during the winter.

But as long as the shelter was there, or even in our imaginations after it was destroyed, we thought the sky could turn to fire at any time and burn away the face of the earth.

When hydrogen bombs and the Cold War came later, I worried about whether or not there would be room for me and my mom in a shelter that sat only fifty. I figured my dad, being a manager and all, would *definitely* have a spot, but I didn't know if he could bring us along. We didn't have the money to build a fallout shelter like some people in my neighborhood erected in the 1950s from free plans the post office gave out, so I didn't know what I'd do if Firestone turned me away when I needed to hide. The safety toes and safety lenses just wouldn't be enough, that I was sure of.

We had duck-and-cover drills in elementary school. *They* made me nervous too. We'd have to go down by our lockers, sit on the floor facing cold gray metal, and put our heads between our knees. We cradled our skulls with our hands to keep the bomb fragments from liberating our brains. There never was any real danger, just like our fire drills. No fires ever started. No hydrogen bombs ever fell.

Still, things were not quite right. The school siren and the cold metal on my nose from the lockers, the shelter that I thought about all the time, even the imaginary tiger and imaginary bombs—all these things made my fragile nerves creep up through my skin, like sprouts looking for the light.

I was like my dad in a way. Trouble had to get closer to my skin, and prick or cut, before I *really* noticed it was there. When changes in my little world became *visible,* or left a mark—that was when I *really* was afraid.

What happened to the trees in the Park—*my* trees—disturbed me more than the thought of our nation being vaporized into a mushroom cloud.

In the 1950s and 1960s, Dutch Elm disease hit the American Elms all over Akron. Akron was a city of elms. Their beauty made me love them, or maybe it was my uncle Paul who did.

Uncle Paul was the one who taught me how to look at trees. My dad never loved nature the way my cousin Paul's dad did. Dad trimmed his bushes and cut his grass because it looked good that way and he was proud of his property. But not my uncle Paul. He sat for hours on a cushion weeding dandelions, planted blackberry and blueberry bushes on the side of his garage, propped tomatoes and rhubarb up with pieces of wood he cut in his cellar, and never bought a power mower.

He invented sayings about plants and weather, and made us laugh.

"Think the rain'll hurt the rhubarb?" I can hear him say.

"No, but it'll beat heck out o' the lettuce," I'd answer, the way he taught me to. I loved the word "heck," and his letting me say it, because I knew it stood for "hell," and I knew he was letting me go someplace with language that I'd never been before.

"Won't be long now—" he'd say, pushing his hand mower.

"Said the monkey who caught his tail in a lawnmower," I'd answer, following behind him with a rake.

"There's a flock of turtles!" he'd yell out, pointing at doves flying toward a phone line.

"They go pretty fast," I'd respond.

There were things Uncle Paul refused to let us do—like watch *American Bandstand* and *Divorce Court* after school or throw ketchup on each other to make blood when we played war or fought with plastic swords. (What we *really* liked to do was convince some new kid in the neighborhood to lie in the street and pretend he'd been hit by a car. We'd lather him up with ketchup and wait to see what the next driver on the road would do when he spotted the body.)

But there were no boundaries on language (except you couldn't write *Xmas* because *that took Christ out of Christmas,* he said). He let us roam, and he broke all the rules himself as he constantly invented funny phrases or mixed English with broken German and carny talk (a code language he'd learned from carnival people). If he hadn't had to work all those years in a rubber plant, I think he would have been a linguist, or a writer.

Uncle Paul was as curious about nature—and the weather—as he was about language. He was eighty-nine when he died and kept a journal most of his life. He never forgot to record the weather. Two wavy columns, penciled in by Uncle Paul, ran down every page of his journals: one for the high of the day, one for the low. He made his last entry the late summer day he broke his hip—an accident that led all the way to pneumonia and death. He wrote just this, "Thunder and Lightning and Rain," and recorded a high of 91 and a low of 69.

To my dad, the apple tree in our backyard was nothing more than a jungle gym for me, and a nuisance for him, with the rotten fruit it dropped always clogging up his gas mower. But my uncle saw curves and color in every tree. If a tree within the sight line of his house had been uprooted and planted on another street, in another state, he could have found it.

My uncle Paul and I would sit on his porch on Ivy Place and look across the street at the most beautiful tree in the world. An American Elm. We needed nothing but that tree to entertain us for an entire afternoon. We watched the shadows its huge branches formed on the house and my uncle always said its gray bark was like an animal, and the furrows like the ridges in its skin. In his hand he'd hold an elm leaf that he found on the ground, and he'd make me feel the veins, the teeth on the edge, the soft hairs underneath on the pale side, until it seemed to come alive as I stroked it in my palm. When I walked home from his house, I would stare into the sun through the canopy of other elms above me. Sometimes, at night, I'd see elm branches in the veins of my own eyes.

Harvey Firestone Sr. ordered the elms to be planted everywhere in Firestone Park, but the trees lost the fight—every single one of them. I'd notice that the leaves would wilt, and next they'd all turn yellow—almost overnight—not *naturally* yellow the way they had every fall. Men in city uniforms would come and cut them down, and I'd hear saws chewing into wood, the pitch growing higher and higher the closer they came to the center of each tree. I'd see the workers on my way to school, and then on my way back home the men would all be gone, and so would the trees.

I stood silently on the playground and pulled the corners of my eyes way back with my fingers to see if I could spot the workers from the sound of saws that told me they were there.

The Park didn't feel as private anymore, after the trees were gone, and even the breeze felt different when it struck directly at my face, without the filter of elm leaves.

I was always thin, and felt vulnerable to strong winds in the spring and sun in the summer. Even insect bites made my skin puff up and stay that way for days. If something like Dutch Elm disease could invade the Park—could kill *trees* that once had seemed so solid and so permanent—what chance did *I* have, their frail sister?

I started to worry about the apple tree in my backyard. I thought the bark beetles that everyone was talking about, those tiny creatures that carried the fungus spores that clogged the vessels of the elms and finally killed them, might also like the taste of apple bark and cause *my* tree to die. It made sense to me that beetles would hunt for apple trees when all the elms were gone. Surely they'd be hungry after killing all those giant trees.

When a single leaf would yellow on the apple tree, I would rush to pull it off, thinking that a yellow leaf was a sure sign of a tree's imminent death, and if I could just remove it, the tree would never die.

Every day the trees in our community were thinning out. Honey Locust and European Hornbeam and Green Ash were planted where American Elms once had been. There were still many of the Park's original trees left standing—Horse Chestnut, Ginkgo, American Yellowwood, Sycamore Maple, Northern Catalpa. We plucked their leaves for our leaf collections at school, and were glad that they were there. But nothing *ever* took the place of the American Elms that disappeared.

The Park just didn't feel as safe after the elms were gone.

≈≈≈

Our *trees* had died, but *we* hadn't. And that was sort of a miracle because it was hard for children to stay alive in the 1940s and 1950s. Polio hovered over the rest of Akron, and the nation, but for a long time kids in Firestone Park seemed immune. For a long while no one talked about cases in the Park, so even though the trees were gone *we* still felt safe. Children in our school occasionally had carbuncles, even lice, but not polio. One boy who sat in front of me had huge pimples on his neck that sometimes oozed and I'd watch him reach for them and squeeze them until they popped. The whole thing made me gag, but I knew it wasn't polio.

Polio was romantic for a while. These were the glory years of the March of Dimes. Howdy Doody supported the cause, and some of us in the Peanut Gallery dreamed of gaining fame by being next year's Poster Child. I sometimes imagined myself crippled, standing with braces on my legs, looking from the poster at the whole world with huge, sad eyes. A caption under me read, "Help Me Walk Again!" I dreamed that people would love me and give money and I'd be cured and become a famous dancer—a ballerina, maybe—and perform in towns in every state on stages just like the one in the auditorium of Firestone Park Elementary School, only bigger.

There were warnings about polio, of course. *Don't play in puddles after it rains. Avoid fatigue. Don't touch your mouth to the water fountain. Stay away from crowds and strangers. Avoid chills and don't bathe too long in cold water. Don't lie down on a warm sidewalk after running through a sprinkler. Don't swim. Don't go to amusement parks. Don't get your tonsils out. Sleep with the windows closed. Sleep with the windows open.* The Lyn Theater on Waterloo Road closed sometimes, and once or twice school let out in the middle of the day. But I knew *I'd* never really get sick. I lived in *Firestone Park,* after all, and I wore safety shoes and safety glasses and my father worked for the Firestone Tire & Rubber Company and there was a Christmas Party every year and all the kids were invited and it just wouldn't be right if I got polio and couldn't go.

Of course I eventually discovered that sometimes children in the Park *did* get sick. They started vanishing for months, or not coming back to school. But polio didn't seem so bad, even then. One girl on the Boulevard took voice lessons to build up her diaphragm after the disease did its damage and became a great singer and was featured on the *Horace Heidt Polio Show* on TV. This reinforced my fantasy of one day being the National Polio Ballerina. You could be on TV or the radio or get your picture in the *Akron Beacon Journal* or *Non-Skid* if you got polio. First you got polio, then you climbed into an iron lung for a while (which looked like a lot of fun to me—even more fun than playing elevator in a hotel closet, which was great), recovered, and then became famous. That's how I thought it worked.

But when my cousin Carol got sick, I realized I'd left things out.

∾✿∾

It was early fall, and I was just beginning to sense how much I liked Miss Wilson, my first-grade teacher. But one morning my mother showed up at the classroom door and made me go with her—more important, made me *leave* Miss Wilson. Annabelle Coyne actually was friends with Miss Wilson, and they took me with them to a restaurant once, where they sipped martinis and sucked olives on sticks the way I would green suckers. I was allowed to order a Shirley Temple—a fruit and soda "drink" for kids—and tried to suck my cherry the way they did their olives, but the temptation was too great to bite right into it and it made only a couple of passes through my mouth before it was gone. I was a little disappointed in Miss Wilson after our trip to the restaurant—after I learned she loved martinis—but I knew I had a huge secret, too. It was all I could do to not call my teacher "Vivien" in class after that.

"Yes, *Vivien,* I'll bring my spelling quiz up to your desk."

"You look so pretty today, *Vivien!* New Toni?"

Well, Vivien Wilson *was* pretty much like family—probably my mom's best friend, except for some of the *girls* at work (she always called them that, "the girls at work," though a few had blue hair and tiny bumps and spots on their necks, like chicken skin). My mother knew I loved Miss Wilson the way *she* did and would never have taken me out of her class without a good reason.

Miss Wilson's first-grade class, author, fourth row, far right

"Carol's sick," is all I remember her saying as she rushed me to our Hudson Hornet. My mother was not a nervous woman, but she was nervous *this* day. I knew something horrible must be wrong, not from what she said about Carol, but from the brittle way she cupped my shoulder and guided me ahead of her. And, most of all, from the way she drove her car. My mother never drove fast in city traffic (it was my dad who got all the tickets in *our* house), but today she was passing everyone and honking the horn—something my *father* liked to do.

We pulled into a parking space by the Second National Building downtown and headed to the seventh floor where our doctor had his office. Dr. Johnson smiled sadly and then said I needed a shot because my cousin had polio and I had played with her the day before. He said I should be thankful there was a shot that helped. I remember thinking that was a stupid thing to say and wondering if J. Walter Johnson had ever had a shot himself, or if doctors never got sick and didn't need them. Just their patients died.

I really didn't understand why I was there. *Carol* was the one who was sick, not me. But I couldn't explain this to anyone because there were too many people talking and nurses were patting my hands and stroking my hair the way they had when my stitches were put in after the lid stuck in my forehead back on Eagle Street. They helped me lower my underpants (I knew what *that* meant). I tried to be brave—closed my eyes, took a deep breath (this was what the nurses said would work, but they were wrong), waited for my fate.

I'll never forget that shot, or how angry I was with Carol for getting polio and taking me out of Miss Wilson's class and causing this needle to be screaming through my flesh. I'm not afraid of shots today, but after that one in the Second National Building it's really a miracle that I don't pass out every time I get a flu shot or even sew a button on. It was worse than the stitches from the can lid. Far worse. I was being given a gamma globulin shot, the only hope for anyone before Jonas Salk made his revolutionary discovery. But I felt *hopeless* as the nurse released what felt like a *quart* of hot fluid into my bony rear.

❧❧❧

Carol was in the hospital for six months, and for the first six weeks of her stay she was quarantined. Her own mother could only stand at her daughter's window and wave. My cousin was just a little girl, and for all that time she would be separated from her mother and her aunts by doctors and nurses and a thick glass wall. And her brother Eddie was dead, and her father was still working at Firestone, but he wasn't coming home anymore, and there was no one left strong enough to pick her up in their arms and rescue her from the terrible place she was in.

Paul Steurer Sr. with Carol King, before Carol's polio

She was there from September to February. Each day nurses placed steaming pads on her body. Each day the odor of her own hot flesh mixed with the odor of sour medicine. Vomit pushed up Carol's throat when she smelled it, and it still does if she thinks about it. One day she was moved to a different floor and given steaming baths instead of compresses.

"Hot as you can stand, dear!" the nurses would plead with her as she first fought the baths, then gave in and let the nurses do whatever they wanted with her.

The epidemic became so severe in Akron that Carol was moved again—this time to the basement of Grace United Church, a huge Romanesque building with domes and towers that stood right beside the hospital, but isn't there anymore. Beds were lined up in rows from wall to wall, sometimes so close that their frames touched, like metal skeletons. There were irrigating stands and linen hampers and an iron lung. What could that small child have thought each morning when she woke up in that unnatural place, where all the children were sick and there were no mothers, and where the sobbing sound of an iron lung replaced the morning radio?

We children were not permitted to visit Carol until she came home. When I first saw her, what shocked me most was that the curl in her hair was gone. She had had the most beautiful brown curly hair I had ever seen. Everyone used to play with it, before she got sick, and she never seemed to mind. It was so beautiful, and there was so much of it, that it seemed like public property. So when Carol's hair grew thin, and the curl grew limp, we felt like something had happened to us too.

Braces were ordered, and therapy. For most of us, life consisted of school, then play. For Carol, there was school, and then the long struggle in the afternoon to learn how to walk again.

It took years before Carol's legs did what she told them to. Her mom, my aunt Marie, never learned how to drive, and you would sometimes see her pulling Carol in a wagon up Grant and down Exchange. As sad as Aunt Marie was about Carol, I think she was happy sometimes that her daughter couldn't walk and she could keep her in that wagon. At least this way Carol wouldn't run across the street and die, the way that Eddie had.

I should have been happy about Carol's recovery, though it was long and slow, and she never got to sing on the *Horace Heidt Polio Show,* though she had a good voice and we all knew it. But I was too afraid for *myself* then to be thankful that Carol had started to walk again.

My terror began after the gamma globulin shot. If it hurt that much *not* to have the disease, I thought, it must be at least a hundred times worse to be like Carol and really *have* it. When I saw my cousin I didn't see a poor creature who had suffered grave sorrow and pain. I only saw a *disease* I knew I didn't want.

I knew this was not a normal illness, the kind that responded to chicken soup and Vicks VapoRub smeared across your chest and then held there with a red cowboy bandanna some grown-up tied around your neck.

The entire time Carol was sick I dreamed at night about waking up paralyzed or losing my legs. Each morning I would touch them and move my toes, happy to feel the life in them, but by evening I began to worry again about falling asleep at night and someone stealing them from me. I feared I would wake up and be like the war veterans I saw downtown, an empty trouser leg flapping next to a crutch, or both legs completely dead, strapped tight to the sides of a wheel-chair.

There was horror here that I couldn't understand. My cousin's hair didn't curl anymore. Her legs didn't work right and the muscles in her calves were gone. She couldn't skate or ride her bike anymore. Everything was wrong, and I hated it. Carol had turned into a little old woman right in front of my eyes, and she'd stopped being fun. I knew she was *really* going to be the Old Maid in the card deck. I couldn't see ahead to the day when she would dance and skate again, and run the bases on a softball team.

Harvey's kingdom was not safe anymore, not the haven Tom Coyne had promised it would be, and surely not the heaven I'd seen the day we arrived. I had forgotten that the only ticket into heaven is death.

But the evil specters I sensed hovered there were *never* after me, though I thought they were.

They were looking for my dad.

"Bur-UP"

Right before the Rededication I looked at old company photographs displayed in the Firestone Service Store by Plant 1. We had bought our Firestone tires in that store with our discount card when I was young, but tonight it had been transformed into a museum. Walls were covered with photographs of Firestone history, mounted perfectly and displayed with dates and captions.

There were several shots of Harvey camping in the woods with Thomas Edison, John Burroughs, and Henry Ford—all of them dressed in suits. The original Scotch pines planted around the statue were chosen to symbolize Edison, Ford, and Firestone.

Harvey must have been a forceful friend, because even a genius like Edison seemed to lose his mind temporarily when he was under Harvey's influence. Edison became obsessed with the idea of America being able to produce its own rubber and late in his life turned botanist, testing 2,300 different plants for latex. He actually formed the Edison Botanic Research Corporation, and Firestone, Edison, and Ford—joined once more—became its stockholders. Edison decided that goldenrod, with a four percent rubber content, was the most promising plant in America. A Firestone biographer tells the story of Harvey making a bedside visit to Edison when he was dying, Edison so weak that the only thing he could do was roll his eyes toward four pieces of vulcanized goldenrod. His final trophies.

Right next to the camping shot was a picture of Harvey and Idabelle with two of their children, all four sitting in front of Harbel Manor. Idabelle was dressed in furs and silver buckles, with a twelve-inch peacock plume sprouting from her hat.

There were other photographs of Firestone factories and employees. One showed women standing proudly beside a huge rubber lifeboat the company had manufactured during the war.

Another showed a whole line of men checking tires by turning them on steel spindles. I mainly saw their backs—sometimes the sharp edges of a profile—but I tried to imagine the sound inside that room, and what the men's faces looked like on the other side of the photograph. I stared at each worker, looking for the curve of my father's neck. Only seldom did the workers peek over their shoulders at the camera. It was dangerous to do something like that with heavy presses in front of them and hot tires swinging in the air, like enormous—deadly—blooms in a Firestone hothouse.

So many of those photos seemed like family photographs. I closed my eyes and could smell rubber in the room. It was my father's smell. I found myself breathing so deeply that I could hear the sound of the air dragging up into my nostrils and feel my chest pushing out unnaturally from the force of the strong cologne that I'd breathed in—breathed so many times before.

There was one picture of the Xylos Rubber Company taken in 1973 that I couldn't stop looking at. The last standing section of my father's reclaim plant was being struck with a wrecking ball that dangled from a cable on a huge crane. Parts of the structure had vaporized, but the girders of one side, like ribs over a lung, remained. I saw the wrecking ball crashing right into my father's side when I looked at the photograph, girders and ribs indistinguishable now.

The picture made me remember Tom Coyne's last years at Xylos, though I really hadn't wanted to.

CHAPTER 10

⁂

"Bur-UP."

In the early 1960s, my dad began to burp. He woke up burping, burped all through the day, burped during dinner, then burped in bed with the radio on. At first he apologized, but gradually the burps became so common, and they seemed so impossible to prevent, that no one said a thing. They were no more distracting to my mom and me than the clock on our Firestone stove that occasionally made a funny buzzing sound between the ticks of its hands.

Before too long, I noticed that my dad would grab his stomach when a really forceful burp worked its way out of him. I could see him wince when this happened, see his neck tighten and his Adam's apple push higher up his throat. He would reach under his shirt and rub his belly, kneading it the way Fred the baker did when he made rye bread on Aster Avenue. The pain seemed to calm down on the weekends—at least Dad kept his hands at his sides a little more—but when Monday rolled around his digestion was as bad as ever.

He was always trying the latest antacid. Rows and rows of pills and chalky tablets were lined up in the deep cabinet Harvey's architect had cut into the upstairs hall of our little Tudor house. When my mother served her stuffed peppers on Saturday night, my dad's first stop after dinner was that cabinet. He took a handful of tablets and chewed them, leaning against the wall in the hallway like a beggar braced against a downtown alleyway. After a while, when the burps got worse, my dad would shake his head when the peppers appeared. "I shouldn't! I *know* I shouldn't, Annabelle! But I *love* your peppers," he said. He loved everything about them, including their smell as they boiled on the stove all Saturday afternoon.

My mother was a terrible cook, but her stuffed peppers rivaled those at Akron's best greasy spoons. The day she stopped serving them—all that rice and meat and all those tomatoes oozing through pepper skins—I knew my dad's stomach was the cause.

If we were eating at a restaurant, my mother issued a warning when she saw Tom Coyne hide behind his menu, on the prowl for beans and spicy food. "You're going to pay, Tommy!" she'd tell him.

My mother gave my father words like these in place of her peppers. She said them in a soprano voice so high it was like a small cry.

My dad was a bass, and he seldom followed the high line of my mother's voice. He loved thick chili and navy bean soup, and they were the first things his eye went to when we ate out. He would eat hot food when he was depressed, and ignore my mother's warnings.

And he would pay, just the way my mom said he would.

After we returned home from watching Tom Coyne eat all the wrong foods at one of his favorite spots, my mother would disappear down the basement stairs to wash out some clothes, and I would run upstairs to do my homework. Dad would stay by himself in the living room. He'd stretch out on his sofa and wait for the pain to begin in his gut again, and then it would start.

"Bur-UP."

≈≈≈

One Saturday morning it was my turn to clean the bathroom. We only had one. Upstairs. My dad had just showered. As usual, water was splashed all over the sink and the linoleum floor. I cleaned up his mess, the way my mother taught me to, and then lifted the seat of the toilet so I could clean it next. My father's stool hadn't flushed, something that happened a lot in a house where there was just one toilet and narrow drain pipes.

I reached for the handle and pressed down. As the water began to swirl, I noticed small threads of blood in the pool. Little bubbles of blood spun near the threads, like ruby beads. I knew immediately that the blood was connected to my father's burps, and I was frightened to death for him, and for myself.

My father explained the medical part to me when I found the courage to ask him about the blood later that afternoon, and kept me informed about his health for the rest of his life. He was always very comfortable with physical things, and it was almost as if he were just waiting for me to ask. *I* was the one who hated blood, not T. W. Coyne.

Before the burps, which he always knew was a sign of illness, Tom Coyne never apologized for his body. He enjoyed it and seemed to think the rest of the world would too. He picked his nose shamelessly, almost with glee. He liked to feel the metal from his Norelco razor tingle his skin as he rolled it over his cheeks, and to empty mounds of whiskers onto the sill after each shave was over. You could just tell from watching him that he loved the touch and color of human dust.

Dad had diverticulitis, he told me that day—severe and painful inflammation of the bowel. Just a few months from the day I discovered the blood, doctors would remove several inches of my father's colon. The surgery didn't help, though, and I often wonder why anyone thought it would. Tom Coyne soon became weak and dehydrated again, collapsing on his sofa after work and sometimes staying there all night. His snores mixed with the drone of the test pattern on the TV, and I'd turn my own radio on to drown out both the TV and my dad.

But he refused to miss a day of work, and never did. Not in thir-

T. W. Coyne on his sofa in the 1960s

ty-seven years. In the morning he draped himself in diapers my
mother made for him because even that short trip down Main to
Emerling and Xylos was unsafe now.

One day he came home from work and announced at dinner
(which he now ate on the sofa off a metal TV tray) that he was going
to die if he couldn't find a way to keep the life inside of him. That's
just the way he said it. *The life inside of me.* We all knew what to do,
programmed all our lives for this. The Cleveland Clinic was an hour
away, and although we'd never been there, we always knew—the way
people in Akron *still* know—that the clinic is everyone's last hope.
When you saw a car head out of the Park toward the clinic, you
knew a man or woman—sometimes even a child—had one more
chance.

The Coynes left their house together, the three of them, and
headed north. My mother drove.

The Cleveland Clinic saved my father's life.

"They've got colored lines on the floor," he told us, impressed by how easy it was for him to find his way around in that enormous complex, and too proud to say what he really meant, that the clinic had rescued him. "With arrows!"

Tom Coyne was given sulfa and steroids and a pack of needles. For several months he shot a needle directly into his leg each evening right before the news.

He was never completely well again after the burps started. I can still see him squeeze that belly and utter the great, sad "Gee whiz!" that became his trademark. But clinic doctors kept the life inside him, just the way he asked them to.

≈≈≈

My dad never told me that his illness coincided with what was going on at Firestone. Unlike the early years, in the 1960s and 1970s he never talked much about the place. I think he knew that Firestone was a part of my life too, the family he had given me with so much pride, the family that had disappointed him so deeply that he couldn't bear to say its name. If he told me what he knew—what he suspected—I might change into an orphan with tangly hair and dark circles under my eyes, because I'd know that Harvey had forgotten me too.

I noticed changes in my father other than his health. But these decades were a *time* of change, and the changes in my dad seemed small to me compared to things like Vietnam and civil rights. He dressed in old brown pants and work shirts in the 1960s before he headed off to Xylos, talked less about buying new cars or "trading up," spent more time scraping dirt from beneath his fingernails with his giant file (big as a ruler), and stopped slicking back his hair with Vitalis. It suddenly turned white.

I can only guess why he told me so little about what happened to him at Firestone in those grave decades. Maybe he didn't understand himself, so it would have been impossible to explain to someone else—especially the daughter he felt responsible for explaining everything to. Maybe he was just trying to survive one more day, one more month, one more year, and there was no opportunity—no energy left—for speculation or reflection. That would be a luxury his *daughter* would have, but he would not. Maybe he thought I was too young, and he was too old, and there was no way to understand this thing together. Perhaps he was just embarrassed, ashamed of himself for falling so short of his dreams.

Sometimes I think he just needed a time of silence in order to gather his strength, the way a fighter rests in a corner before the next brutal round.

Or maybe there was some signal I was giving off that said this didn't interest me right now, or I didn't care to know, or it wasn't important next to the world's problems. Maybe something in my own demeanor said *Daddy, stay away from me with all this trouble.*

In August of 1973, my father retired. He did tell me that. I sent him a card, but there was no party. It was all so different from my grandfather's retirement. Twenty years earlier, when W. T. stepped away, there had been celebrations at Akron's best restaurants and stories in the *Non-Skid*.

There was not even a picture the size of a postage stamp of Tom Coyne in the *Non-Skid* when he left the company he'd served for thirty-seven years.

After Tom Coyne died in 1990, in a two-drawer file cabinet I found a manila folder that contained a series of memos and letters from the 1950s and 1960s. Those stray bits of paper sketched the history of those years with Firestone, as well as I will ever know them.

Letters were missing, but what *was* there allowed me to begin to understand what made the lining of my father's body burn away.

T. W. Coyne was a packrat, so those papers he left may not have been meant for me. But I like to think they were. I like to think my father knew that one day I would find that manila folder with the gold label—the single word *Firestone* typed on it by my mother years and years before with the old Royal upright that sat in the back room of our Evergreen Avenue house.

That one day I would want to understand.

I like to think he knew what I would find, and that he meant for me to find it.

That this was both my test—a final quiz he would place on my bed before I went to sleep at night—and his hard gift.

I like to think that folder waited just for me. It was *always* waiting. Waiting for time to pass, for Tom Coyne to die, for his daughter to leave the Park and make her own mistakes, for her to learn how to miss him, for age and sorrow and death to teach that little girl how to *read* the papers she would find the summer that she buried Mr. Coyne in the ground of Holy Cross Cemetery in Firestone Park.

That folder had waited all those years, and so had he.

CHAPTER 11

⁀꙰⁀

My dad loved Richard Milhaus Nixon. Not as much as he had loved Harvey Firestone Sr., of course, but he *did* love Nixon. Nixon was a navy man, chosen by Eisenhower, and Eisenhower's vice president from 1953 to 1961—perhaps the happiest years of my father's life. Maybe that's really why T. W. Coyne liked him the way he did. My father didn't speak for days after Kennedy defeated Nixon in 1960. Nixon was like a brother to him, only two years younger than my father. He even looked a little like my dad, with those big bulldog jowls and that toothy grin. Nixon was tough on Communists. Tough on crime. And, like my dad, he wasn't any *union* man. He sided with the country's managers, the way Tom Coyne had been taught to do.

The largest single day's production in twenty years at the Xylos Rubber Company was recorded in 1961—by Tom Coyne. A month before, under his management, the plant had turned in the lowest percentage of product rejections in Firestone's reclaim history. He put these things in a memo to company executives, the last one he would ever write to them.

Increasing pounds per man was the motto of middle managers like my dad. If Firestone said performance could be improved by giving each man more work to do, Tom Coyne believed the company and set out to *use his brain,* the way it taught him. Began to figure this hard thing out.

Use your brain. That was my father's credo. I sometimes think that Harvey whispered it into Tom Coyne's ear the day they met.

Right after stumbling through the prayer on holidays, my dad told about that meeting with the great Harvey Firestone. The story and the prayer always came after a stiff Manhattan.

T. W. Coyne had actually *known* Harvey Firestone Sr. He had *spoken* to the man. Harvey and Tom Coyne had had a conversation. For the first two years of his employment—from 1936 to 1938—my father could brag that he *worked* for Harvey Firestone Sr., worked for the great man himself. And he never missed a chance for a brag.

I can almost see him in his Goosetown drive with one hand on his Ford V-8, the other in the pocket of his double-breasted suit coat, his curly hair slicked back, smiling as wide as the chrome grille on his car, hoping someone would walk by so he could wet his lips and say he worked for Mr. Firestone—then tell the *what, when, who, why, where* and all of it, just the way he would in his speeches. The stranger would tilt his hat and shake Dad's hand.

Holidays were the only time my father drank at home (my mother hated him to drag vermouth and whiskey from the upper shelf), and he always made Manhattans. The drink loosened him up right away and made him feel good and laugh a lot. It stirred awake the story of the day he met the founder, who may as well have been my father's maker too.

My young father had gone up to the third floor of the main plant to view a service exhibit. T. W. had worked at service stations before joining the Firestone staff, pumping gas and fixing cars, but he had never seen anything like the repair exhibit on display that day. My father couldn't help smiling.

"What do you think of it, son?" an old man standing behind him said.

"It's swell!"

That was the end of it. Two lines exchanged on a factory floor.

"Guess who that man was?" my father would ask each time he told his story, leaning way back in his chair and hooking his thumbs through his belt.

"Who, Dad?" I said.

"Who was it, Tommy?"

"Who, Dad?"

It would have broken his heart if my mom and I had failed to feign surprise at the answer he always gave.

He often alternated this story with one other—his memory of Mr. Firestone's last visit to Plant 1 in 1938. When my father's whiskey completely settled in, usually toward the end of a long, heavy dinner, he grew sad and teary-eyed. He jumped at times like this to 1938.

He didn't tell the *whole* story of that year, of course. He didn't tell about the major strikes in Akron's rubber industry, involving over four thousand men and terrible violence. He left things out because he loved Mr. Firestone and love had made him blind, the way it almost always does.

He remembered Harvey's body being returned by train from Miami ("By *train!*" he said, never quite believing it, because the black hearse at Schermesser's Funeral Home in the Park was the only thing my dad had ever seen the dead ride in). He had died at Harbel Villa in Florida, but was brought back to Akron and then taken to the ground floor of Plant 1 so his workers could say goodbye. My father and my grandfather were there that day, and they paraded right past the bier, right by Harvey's rich bronze casket, and shook their heads, not knowing what to think or say.

"Flags were at half-mast," was the line my father always ended with, always a little catch in his throat.

Yes, sir, the whole town lowered its flags that day.

❧❧❧

Somewhere along the way, the company decided it could not feel the same affection for Tom Coyne that Tom Coyne felt for Firestone. For a long time he would practically salute the neon *F* whenever we'd drive down Main Street and see those Firestone signs glowing on the roofs of Plant 1 and Plant 2. My father decorated his lapels with Firestone pins, bought only Firestone products for his car and home (including a wringer washer that nearly took my mother's arm off), and kept Firestone time with the Bulova wristwatch the company gave to him (the Bulova came after the twenty-year pocket watch, and was incorrectly inscribed to Tom Cohn).

One day in 1962, my dad was told that because he had only a high-school diploma, he was going to be demoted. He had the choice of becoming a fourth-shift foreman or moving to the personnel department. He was not *promotable* without a college degree. His salary would necessarily also be reduced, *you certainly will understand, Tom.* I have the letter that gave him the news. It's printed on a piece of Firestone stationery.

I also have the memo he wrote in response, the memo that begins by citing his proud accomplishments at Xylos. It's a carbon paper copy, difficult to read, but my father was pressing down hard the day he composed it and it's all still there.

"It is with great emotional turmoil and a sorrowful heart that I say I cannot understand this treatment." There would be no more memos after this. "Perhaps a college degree would give me the understanding I need to comprehend what you have done," my father concluded, in a line so bold I watch him jump out of his Firestone skin into something else every time I read it.

My father ended up staying at Xylos as a fourth-shift foreman—no longer production manager—without any hope of ever being plant manager. He eventually was given a better shift, and then be-

Tires on shipping dock, ready for reclaim, Xylos, 1932
(Courtesy of Bridgestone/Firestone, Inc.)

fore long was demoted again. By the end of the decade he was a lower-level supervisor in shipping and receiving and worked mainly on the loading dock.

Tom Coyne began wearing colored shirts instead of white and carrying his lunch (with a little change for the vending machine), instead of eating in the Firestone Clubhouse. He started to gain weight, and look old.

His desk was hauled away.

He began to burp.

He must have wondered where things went wrong. Weren't the classes he had struggled through designed to help him be "promotable"? Mostly middle managers took those courses and then one day they disappeared into upper management and never came to class again, just walked out and left an empty seat right beside my dad, who was *always* there, and never disappeared. Why had he never been picked, and why had Firestone told him to *use his brain,* and why had he tried everything they said and taken all those classes and made trips to other reclaim plants in Pennsylvania to get ideas for equipment and production, and it *never* was enough?

How could he have been so foolish to think a place as dangerous as Xylos was, a place of mills and knives and sulfur fumes, could be safe for *him?* He surely knew the shiny black tires that left the show-room would inevitably be dumped onto the Xylos lot. Day after day, how had he missed the resemblance between the torn tread on those old tires and his own aging skin? Had his weak right eye failed him so entirely?

He was in *reclaim,* after all. He knew what happened when things got old, because it was his *job* to know. How had this gum-dipped man failed to see that the company would one day shred him too, the way they shredded their tires?

He had thought that Firestone was a place where things hap-pened in intervals of centuries, the way the large words promised on the Firestone Memorial. *What the centuries said, as against the years and as against the hours,* we read together all those Sundays of my youth. He thought Harvey had a noble plan for him, for his *entire life,* all the length and breadth of it.

He had forgotten to remember *seconds* anymore. I'm sure my fa-ther thought that seconds were for union men with timecards, not for men like him.

But in a *second,* the time it takes to rip the seal open on an enve-lope, everything had changed.

CHAPTER 12

❧❧❧

I don't know how it was decided that my dad wasn't good enough to manage Xylos, but I think about this all the time. I want to understand. I want to see the complications.

Maybe the superintendent of Xylos just didn't like him. Maybe it was as simple as that. My dad was not the easiest person to really *like,* after all. My aunts certainly felt that way.

He was the least popular man in our whole family, and that was saying something. We had our share of alcoholics, cowards, and reckless men. It made perfect sense to me that Dr. Bob Smith and Bill Wilson, two alcoholics, founded Alcoholics Anonymous in 1935 in *Akron.* Akron was a hard-drinking town, and my family was part of that tradition. Dr. Bob's home on Ardmore Avenue is a National Historical Landmark now, and was a halfway home for alcoholics during his lifetime. I only wish some of the men in my family had known about Dr. Bob and about that house. I don't think they ever did.

My father had a weakness for alcohol too, but most of the time he kept it under control. *Most* of the time. Once in a while the owner of a bar and grill near our house had to call our home and ask my mom to come get Dad. My mother's cheeks would turn bright red when she heard the voice on the phone, but she'd faithfully walk the long blocks to the restaurant no matter what time the owner phoned. Tom Coyne loved to go out on Fridays after work to "talk business" with the other men from Xylos. Just two Manhattans and his voice became louder than the jukebox that took his change.

Sometimes the men from the plant went to a downtown bar. Then there was no call and Dad ended up driving home alone. More than once he crunched our Plymouth or Chrysler swerving down the streets of Akron looking for the driveway to his little Tudor house.

More than anything, though, I think my father wanted to make my mom and me happy, so most of his energy went into keeping our house in good repair, not drinking Manhattans. I knew he hated trimming that privet hedge of ours, but he did it anyway. And he continually patched the trellis where our purple clematis grew, as if a single rotten board could somehow ruin everything. He hated the apple tree in the backyard a little more each year, but he knew I liked it so he let it stay. I sometimes don't know if it was the house that made us happy all those years, or my father's vow to keep it perfect for us.

But sometimes my father just tried too hard. People didn't like that, or understand it the way my mother and I grew to. Tom Coyne never had an easy way with kids, the way my uncle Paul always did. Uncle Paul could charm us right into his arms. My dad couldn't even hold us right. We dangled over his elbows and screamed to be put down, though this perplexed him and made him sad. Even when my own son was young, Tom Coyne would sit him on his sofa and tease and tickle him like a doll, rather than risk holding him in his awkward arms.

He wasn't funny, either, though he thought he was and always laughed at everything he said and everything he heard that had a funny twist to it. He depended on jokes from the *Reader's Digest* or the *Akron Beacon Journal,* trying out the Joke for the Day at the

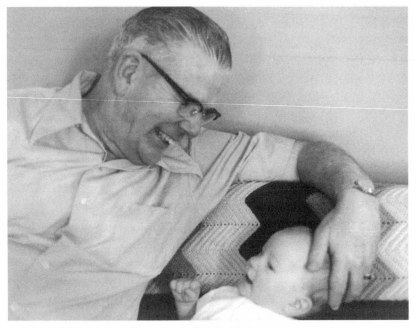

T. W. Coyne with grandson, Stephen Osborn Dyer, on sofa, 1972

breakfast table—rehearsing it—then taking it to work for his men. He always had a joke to tell, swinging his arms as he delivered it and moving his feet in a little dance.

My dad was the family clown, the way he'd been in high school. But no one thought he was funny. I didn't always listen to him when he told his joke from the morning paper. I pretended that oatmeal was the most interesting thing on earth and stared into my bowl.

And he tried too hard to be interesting. He was so conscious of the need to have something important to say that he interrupted everyone with stray facts he'd picked up from the radio or his *Read-*

er's Digest or the daily crossword puzzle he'd worked. We all knew he wasn't interesting, at least not the way my aunt Marie's boyfriend was, or my uncle Steve. *They* were always talking about books—*real* books—and art and music. And *they* had degrees from Akron University, not just public speaking courses sponsored by some company, and Uncle Steve wore bow ties. My father *wanted* to be like them, but he just *wasn't*.

In a high-school picture his senior year, my dad stands in a back row of bleachers with a letter sweater on (oddly, part of the *S* on the front—for South High—is blocked out by the person in front of him, and it looks like a Firestone *F*). He has his hands draped over the shoulders of the boy in the row below him, almost as if my father needs to document his easy way with people. The overweight boy receiving my father's attentions has his mouth wide open, perhaps forming the words, *Coyne, get your goddamn hands off me!* It may have annoyed the boy that he had to stand straight for the picture and couldn't reach around and belt my dad.

Tom Coyne was a carouser when he was young, a boy who always stayed out late and liked to have fun, but never really knew how to do that either. He played a saxophone—silver-plated—and was in a dance band. He was on the football team, too, but seldom made it to the field. They let him wear a uniform, so it didn't matter much to Tom Coyne if he played or not. I see him there, becoming a Firestone man even then. Giving people what they wanted, so maybe they'd want *him*.

At Xylos I'm sure he acted the same way he did in high school, and the same way he did around our family. He may have laughed too loudly in the morning when men were just waking up, shared the Daily Chuckle in the restroom before people were ready to hear it, slapped a manager a little too hard on the back in a business meet-

T. W. Coyne with his silver saxophone, 1925

ing. Bragged too much and bored his men with obscure facts about coins or Big Bands or Central American rivers—words that fit in three-down or four-across.

My father wanted to be king of the dance in high school, and plant manager at work. He wanted to be photographed sitting on a crescent moon at Summit Beach Park with his sweetheart, Annabelle Coyne, or receiving safety awards at Xylos. He wanted to make his family unspeakably happy in the little Tudor house he had bought for them.

He wanted someone, just once, to tell him he had done something right.

❧❧

Or maybe it was his tendency to always make a mess that did him in. He was famous in our family for dropping clutter everywhere and refusing to throw anything out. He left his dirty handkerchiefs on tables and countertops, glued shut with yellow goo. We'd pick them up by a clean corner and walk them down to the basement at arm's length to my mother's tub of bleach, as silver as Dad's saxophone.

There were always clothes around his bed, the bathroom tile came unglued because he splashed so much, clippings from toenails piled up on the rug right under the sill full of whisker dust, and his books and change were scattered all over the coffee table and TV top.

There were no centerpieces in our house, no nice spring sprays of flowers. Within minutes of their arrival on any surface, Dad would cover them completely with debris from his pockets, and bury them.

A Xylos manager wrote a memo to my dad early in his career when he was working night shift. It was one of the things he'd stored in the folder that I found. Tom Coyne was praised for an excellent job getting devulcanizers loaded. *Your production gets better every night,* his boss wrote. But was *this* the real message, or was it the small note that followed the commendation: *P. S. Be careful not to cover any men up with stock on the fifth floor, Tom!*

His supervisor seemed amused by my dad's excesses, but the sarcasm was beginning. I heard the same slight irritation in that line that I heard in my aunts' voices when they talked to my mom about my dad's slovenly ways. About how Annabelle shouldn't tolerate his constant mess.

My mother turned deaf when they said these things to her.

I can see the stacks of tires and scrap forming a sort of warren under my father's rule, and the workers becoming smaller and smaller and having a harder and harder time maneuvering. This was the kingdom my father would create. I can see the men grow smaller as the rubber walls on either side grow taller and wider, until the men finally vanish from view and disappear. I hear a muted shout as they call for someone—for anyone—*to get them out!* My father blows his silver saxophone, leaps in the air, sails over a stack, and leads his men away, tooting "Walkin' My Baby Back Home," swinging those bony hips.

They cheer for him.

✱✱✱

But it was the bragging that *really* got on everyone's nerves. I'm pretty sure the letter had something to do with my father's tendency to brag.

Tom Coyne was proud of his performance record and his safety awards, as his memo showed. He was *always* bragging about his plant. If his superiors read his pride as arrogance, this may have been enough to make them want to level him, to flatten him on his own mill. Maybe they thought he was taking too much credit for himself.

The bragging didn't stop with Xylos. My cousins and I were often the cause of it. I noticed it got worse in my high-school years, a time, I realize now, that coincided with Tom Coyne's first demotion.

My father sat in the front row of all the school plays I was ever in, and may as well have brought his silver saxophone and blown it, for all the noise he made when I stepped on stage. He would brag about Paul and Carol and Joyce everywhere he went, and to anyone who would listen. And he especially bragged about Joyce.

He was a regular at Krispy Kreme on the weekends and after work and could usually find a stranger who would listen to him for a cup of coffee and one sugar glazed. It didn't matter if anyone *really* listened, and they usually didn't. What mattered was simply that the words were released into the air, and he could hear them. He bragged to friends, neighbors, doctors and dentists, people in the post office, tellers in the bank, store cashiers, butchers, shoe repairmen, waitresses, priests and ministers, the paint and decorating man, a salesman for Timken Bearing Company, Fred the baker, Leffler at the filling station.

My cousin Paul was going to be a doctor and open up a practice in Akron. *Right in our town!* Carol was on the school newspaper and in the band and orchestra, and oh, her voice, like an angel that voice. He talked about us ceaselessly. When I was with him and he did this kind of thing, I watched the spit bubble from his lips and felt disgust, and wanted to become invisible.

I wasn't a star in science, like my cousin Paul, who always won the Science Fair, but I *was* in plays with *Ray Wise,* and that was almost as good to my father. Ray Wise went to my high school and everyone knew already that Akron's Ray, who lived on Prentiss Avenue, was going to be famous—long before he killed Laura Palmer in David Lynch's *Twin Peaks,* or won important parts in *RoboCop* and *Bob Roberts.* My father must have thought that I had a chance to be famous too if I got the female leads in the plays *Ray* starred in. When Ray and I were taken down to the *Beacon Journal* by our coach Jack McKinney or William Waggoner for publicity shots, I pictured my dad hanging out the window of his plant with a telescope trying to follow us all the way down Main Street.

Little did my poor father realize what a gulf there was on the stage between Ray's talent and my own. He didn't see that no one noticed *me* when Ray was standing there.

Whatever I did was *great* in my father's eyes. After my hair bleached out in the sun one summer, and I traded my blue aluminum frames with rhinestones for contact lenses, boys noticed me for the first time and I was sometimes invited to parties in rec rooms to slow dance and listen to 45s.

But my father didn't care that I was doing a little better on the popularity polls. I don't think he even noticed. The only things—truly the *only* things—that mattered to him about my years in high school were that I got good grades and was in plays.

I think Tom Coyne dreamed about the Firestone Scholarship long before he said anything to me. Dreamed about it every time I showed my grades to him or stepped onto a stage ("extracurricular activities are important," the Firestone Scholarship Committee advised applicants and their eager parents in *Non-Skids*).

Firestone inaugurated its scholarship in the 1950s. Even before that, in the 1920s, Firestone had sponsored essay contests for high-school students on the topic of good roads. Winners won four-year college scholarships, plus expenses, the same prize Firestone Scholarship winners would receive decades later.

Like the annual Christmas party, the scholarship competition was only open to children of employees. But not to all of them. When I applied, if your father or mother earned more than $800 a month, you were ineligible.

Our family qualified because my father had been demoted and made far less money now. I could take the test because my father had lost any chance of advancement for himself.

Ray Wise and author in The Mouse That Roared, *Garfield High School, 1965*

There were eight Firestone Scholarships awarded that year, along with fifty-four Certificates of Merit. One of those eight went to me, and changed my life.

I went to college on the coattails of Tom Coyne's humiliation. *I* was the one, not Tom Coyne, who would receive a letter of congratulations signed by Harvey S. Firestone—even if it was *Jr.,* the "real" Harvey's son. It's a horrible irony I cannot come to peace with, even after all this time. There are *so* many ironies in the Firestone story.

I have a picture of myself standing with other scholarship winners on the patio of the Firestone Country Club on a May afternoon. It was taken right after a lunch in our honor (I'd never set foot on the grounds of the club before). We're standing in two rows that begin on the ground then wind up a set of tall steel stairs, and I'm wearing a sundress with a big white collar and daisies, and white summer gloves. I'm in the front row with one foot far in front of the other, like I'm about to walk out of the photograph. Executives—lots of them— are scattered throughout the lines we form. I look for my father among the men in suits, but he's not there. Of course not. He *can't* be there, or I would have to leave the picture. Step away. He had to be demoted—to be in the background—for me to be in the foreground of this shot. As I look at the picture, I know that I would do anything now, *anything at all,* to dress my father in a suit and place him in this photograph instead of me.

But *would* I? What would that have meant? Nothing would seem to be risked at all if I were to make this one small change. My dad would be the executive he had always hoped to become, and even though I wouldn't qualify to take the scholarship test anymore, his larger salary would have paid for school. But what I fear is that such good fortune would have changed everything, as much as I desire it. It would have changed my father, and it would have changed me. My father might never have discovered what he was really meant to do if his company had loved him the way they said they would. And I may have chosen a path very different from the one I have, chosen a path paved with comfort and silence rather than with this gravelly obsession I have to be heard.

The strength and ambition my father gave me could not have come from his having lived a more successful life, even though I wish that he had had one. He chose to live his life through me because Firestone took his own dreams away, and as guilty as I am to think of it, I know my intensity about so many things begins with my

Firestone Country Club luncheon for Firestone Scholarship winners, 1965

dad. I can trace it right to him. Would my passion for words be as great if Tom Coyne had failed to place those *Reader's Digest* vocabulary quizzes on my bed, knowing we *both* needed them? Where did my wild love of teaching come from, if not from my father who taught me everything he knew, because no one else cared what Tom Coyne had to say? Shy and female, would I have had the confidence I do most days without those blasts of faith from my father's silver saxophone still ringing in my ears? Would I even have chosen to write without my father's stories to tell?

One foot steps away in the picture, and the other is parallel with all the other feet in the Firestone line. I see myself wobble, tilt, move forward and then draw back. But I know it's all an illusion. There is no movement in a photograph. The ambivalence in the pose I strike is the permanent ambivalence I will *always* feel about how the Firestone story has turned out for me. The best I can do is try to walk gracefully in this world without splitting myself in half.

☙☙☙

The day the winners were selected, my father called me from Xylos. It was after school, and he knew I'd be upstairs by the Royal upright starting my homework. It was the only time I can ever remember him phoning home from his plant. Phoning home on company time was just something he thought a good employee shouldn't do. Something *he* shouldn't do. *Wouldn't* do.

There was right and wrong in my father's world in the early decades when his love for Firestone was unqualified. Anything that hurt the company, or took a dime away from it, was just plain wrong. I still hesitate when I call home from the college where I teach. People do it all the time, but it *never* will feel right to me.

I could hear factory noises in the background, but my father's voice was so strong and so loud that it drowned out the whole world of rubber.

"You won, dear Ann!" he yelled in my ear. "You're going to *college!*"

I heard myself gasp *thank you, thank you, Daddy* into the receiver, and wait for what he might say next. I almost expected to hear him blow the silver horn he still took out sometimes and cleaned, but seldom played anymore.

My winning that scholarship was the closest *he* would ever come to being Xylos plant manager at the Firestone Tire & Rubber Company, and I think he knew that when he called.

"They're going to pay for everything!" There was a short pause. I listened hard.

"They're going to pay!" he said again, until the sound of rubber rose where his voice had been, and the phone clicked dead.

"Fraternally Yours, P. Bommarito"

The Centennial Committee had wanted to make the Rededication cere-mony just like the one in 1950. Voice of Firestone *regular Eleanor Steber had sung "Oh God, Our Help in Ages Past" at the original Dedication of Harvey's statue, and now that same hymn was being sung by the Men and Boys Choir of St. Paul's Episcopal Church—Harvey's church when he lived in town.*

We stood as the choir sang. I grew dizzy and felt a cold pain jab through my head, like a needle boring right through the bone of my skull. I saw my grandpa's white hair, and then my dad's. Curls flew everywhere in the breeze and rose in loops and spirals toward the sky.

I steadied myself, and my vision cleared. Long strands of hair shot from the back of my neck. It wasn't the hair of my Firestone ancestors that had blown in front of me, but my own.

After the choir the speakers came.

Kimball Firestone, Harvey's grandson, spoke for his family. Masatoshi Ono, Chairman and CEO of Bridgestone/Firestone, spoke for the compa-ny. Firestone quality and high standards had continued to the present day, he said.

Small children of the Firestone clan were called to the front and given laser lights.

There was no veil on the broad shoulders of the bronze man to pull away this time (though for the occasion Harvey had enjoyed a facelift to chip off fifty years of oxidation that had dribbled down his cheeks), nor were any Firestone sons alive to remove it if it had been there. Instead,

159

laser lights and pyrotechnics were used to dazzle those of us at Harvey's second Dedication—thousands fewer than the ten thousand who attended the first.

The children were instructed to point their laser beams at Harvey, as if they were turning on the power, the way that Harvey Jr. had started up his father's first factory nearly one hundred years before. They weren't looking at the statue the way I had when I was young, with my head bent back so far my brain could have broken from its stem. They stared, instead, at the red dots made by their laser lights ("Cool!" "Cool!" they screamed) and watched the first sparks burst from behind the bronze ancestor they had never known. They were amazed by the explosion they thought they had caused, and we laughed as we watched them being fooled.

Kettledrums began, heralding the fiery celebration above our heads. Blades of silver light shot toward ancient stars, then glittered back to earth. Great waves of blue and green swirled over Harvey's chest and colored honey locusts planted when the Scotch pines died. Leaves and branches waved above us like wings of seraphim, and it was impossible to think that songbirds ever would return to this wild place.

The sound of light exploding in the air, the evening's grand finale, made my heart beat fast, and touch my ribs.

It made me think of Tom Coyne's own exit from the company, and what he must have felt inside.

CHAPTER 13

❦

"Janitor," the clerk read from a 3 x 5 card. We were sitting in an office in Firestone's old Plant 1.

The card with my father's employment record on it showed that he had retired on clock—he'd been an hourly worker, in other words. From a tax form I'd found, I knew he was no longer on salary in the 1970s, but how that had come about was unclear to me. I made an appointment with the Industrial Relations office at Bridgestone/Firestone to find out, thinking they would have details of his employment.

"Your dad worked for Firestone as a janitor, right?" the clerk asked, staring at the card, and then at me.

I can't explain the surprise I felt. I took the card from the man and saw that all the information was correct—social security number, date of birth, everything. Except the job. This was, without question, my father's last record with the company. But it was as if the clerk had found a Tom Coyne I had never known. For nearly twenty years my father had kept hidden from me not only the details about his demotions in management in the 1960s, but also this final fact: He had ended his career in the 1970s as a janitor on clock.

"He was a janitor with the Synthetic Plant when he left Firestone," the clerk repeated. "Department 733."

He was a nice man, this Bridgestone/Firestone clerk, but the information he'd given me about my dad was not what I'd expected, and I could hardly speak. He saw my shock.

161

"Let me look around and see if there's more paperwork on your dad. If there is, I'll call you, OK?"

"Please," I answered, and gave him my phone number. "Please call," I said as I shook the clerk's hand and hurried down the hallway toward the door that led to the lobby. Surely it had to take more than one small card to preserve the record of my father's thirty-seven years with the Firestone Tire & Rubber Company.

But I never heard from the clerk again. Later, after I realized the phone wasn't going to ring, I called the corporate offices in Nashville. T. W. Coyne's name came up on the screen when I gave someone in Human Resources his social security number, but all they had was the date when he started with the company (June 26, 1936), the date he retired, and the date he died. Three dates for thirty-seven years. "Think about it," the officer told me. "It's just been way too long. Anyway, his records never *went* to Nashville. We wouldn't bring them here. We entered the basics into the computer for your dad, but it's impossible to keep everything after someone dies. His records were probably destroyed. Bridgestone/Firestone has North America *and* South America now—80,000 active employees, as well as all those retirees who are still living. We have to clean house." It made perfect sense.

❧❧❧

When I'd entered Akron's Industrial Relations office, I couldn't stop staring at a two-wall exhibit of Firestone memorabilia. But on my way *out* of the building, none of that held my interest any longer. I just wanted to sit in my car and catch my breath.

My dad had retired on August 1, 1973, after almost four decades of service. He had retired as a janitor in the Synthetic Plant.

It's OK, I told myself again and again, bracing my arms against the steering wheel. *It doesn't matter. It doesn't change a thing. Why is this upsetting you?*

It really didn't bother me that my father was a janitor. Why would it? But I knew it would have bothered *him.* That's what I began to think was bothering *me.*

It would have wounded Tom Coyne's pride. He understood the world of the factory the way it had been explained to him when he joined the company in the 1930s. There was a strict hierarchy of laborers, foremen, supervisors, managers, superintendents, and, of course, executives like W. T. At the very *bottom* were janitors, and most of them were black. The *Akron Negro Directory* compiled in 1940 shows angry rows of job labels after names: *student, unemployed, fireman, unemployed, City Garbage Department, Convalescent Home, WPA, Goodyear janitor, unemployed, domestic, unemployed, Firestone janitor, domestic, domestic, janitor, Firestone janitor, rubber worker, Firestone mill man, Goodyear elevator operator, prizefighter, janitor, unemployed.*

I can still hear my father say that janitors wiped the floor because no one was lower than a janitor, and no one was lower than a Negro. He smiled when he said this, but there was something *mean* there too, and I always felt it. It was *unkind,* and all the soft edges of his face turned into hard ridges when he spoke. I never feared my father, except when the word "Negro" perched on his upper lip, and stayed there until his laugh was over and let it down.

I know that someone fed my father the line about Negroes and janitors, along with other phrases he brought home—*pickaninnies* and a *jigaboo Saturday night* were some of his favorites. The fact is, though, that Tom Coyne said them.

What he said about janitors was of course a slur against people he thought were inferior to him. *Negroes.* But it was also connected to his deepest fears about *himself*—to the self-doubt and self-loathing he so often cloaked with flowered shirts, bravado, and a voice that drowned out everyone else's.

Janitor. That single word contained the worst scolding of my father's life. I'm sure that when he heard it a part of him felt like throwing himself before the feet of the Firestone statue or the memory of W. T. and asking for forgiveness. This son of *two* Firestone fathers— W. T. at home, Harvey at work—could surely find forgiveness from one of them, or at least a place to burrow his head so he would never have to see the sun again. I'm sure he was glad his father was dead when this happened to him. How could he have told his father? Surely W. T. would have heard anyway. His phone would have rung one day, or standing in a bank line with another Firestone executive the news would have just slipped out. "Sorry about Tom, W. T.," a friend would have whispered, shaking my grandpa's hand, just the way he would have offered sympathy to the bereaved at a funeral home before viewing the body in the casket.

I wasn't sure how this had happened to my dad when I talked to the Akron clerk, but I knew Firestone had somehow finally won. I understood so much more now about my father's final shame. The company had put him at the very bottom, the way Tom Coyne would have seen it.

He could never tell the truth about his last job with the company because it brought everything into question. No one, I'm sure he thought, would love him anymore. No one could respect a janitor. *He* never had.

What would the family say? My mother's sisters, whose doubts about my father would have been confirmed by this, what would they say? Why would his nephew, the surgeon, listen to his uncle anymore? What would his daughter, who'd been to *college,* think of him?

What had it gotten him to try to *use his brain?* What good had it done to even *have* one if he was pushing a broom around?

He had never found the courage to tell me what had happened to him. He had never let me comfort him. I felt angry thinking of all that he had hid from me. Of what seemed a lack of trust.

But sitting in the Bridgestone/Firestone parking lot, I realized that I was not without blame. I had never asked him about the end of his career. Not when it happened, and not during the many years after it was over. I had never asked for any details. Never asked why there was no retirement dinner at Iacomini's, no party hats and thick steaks like he loved.

I had never really gone out of my way while my father was alive to understand his life—its beginning, *or* its end. My shock at seeing the word *janitor* had less to do with my father's shame than with my own.

How could a daughter not know something like this had happened to her dad? How could she have noticed that he had stopped sweeping the leaves from the floor of his garage one autumn day in the 1970s, but not have wondered *why?* All his life he'd worked to keep it clean with his great push broom, but now the leaves formed enormous nests on every shelf and in every corner.

My neglect seemed to me even worse than what Firestone had done to T. W. Coyne.

I noticed tiny splotches of red forming on my face as I stared in the visor mirror, so I pushed it up and drove away.

CHAPTER 14

From the day I learned my father ended his career as a janitor, I knew I had to find out how a thing like that could have happened.

His demotion to janitor was the *final* scene in the last act of my father's Firestone story, an act that ended with his retirement.

I knew a little about the history of my father's plant, but it took weeks in Akron's archives to find out what I *really* had to know. What I came to see was that the *first* scene in that final act began the day Firestone decided to close the Xylos Rubber Company. That was 1972, the year before my dad retired.

Reclaim was the bastard child of the industry. It recycled the company's failures—tires that wore out, blew out, gave out. It's where the Firestone ATX, ATXII, and Wilderness AT tires would have gone after the 2000 recall if Xylos had still been standing. Xylos had none of the romance of production. It was the afterbirth.

The company blamed the closing on low profit margins and a decreased demand for reclaim. Synthetic rubber was being manufactured cheaply now, cutting even more deeply into the reclaim market.

The union complained that closing Xylos was the company's fault. The company was not willing to invest sufficient money in reclaim to allow Xylos to modernize and become competitive.

But the decision had been made.

And with that decision came one other.

Firestone fired T. W. Coyne.

There was a second folder at the very back of my father's badly damaged file drawer, but I'd ignored it. It was labeled "URW—T. W. Coyne," so I'd just assumed it contained papers from his union years in the 1930s and 1940s—pay stubs, notices about procedures and meetings, things like that. But it was there I found another letter, and the rest of Tom Coyne's story. It was there I found Act 5.

Xylos closed forever, and Tom Coyne was fired. Scene 1, Act 5.

∾∾∾

Since 1962 a series of humiliations had forecast my father's doom. He had been unable to keep pace on the company escalator for at least ten years. In 1972 he had finally lost his footing.

No one had wanted my father around for a long time. His opinion was never solicited, he wasn't invited to dinners or picnics for management, his name stopped appearing under "Xylos News" in the *Non-Skid*s. He had become not much more than a pack mule in his position on the loading docks.

"Treat me like a colored man," I'd sometimes hear him mumble in the hallway as he removed his clothes.

Then with a rag he used to wax the car, he'd wipe the carbon black that streaked his face and neck. "I may as well be one," he'd say.

My dad's remarks sounded more and more offensive to the liberal ears I was beginning to sprout in the 1960s, but I'm beginning to understand that saying those ugly words was his way of finding out what injustice really felt like. His way of imagining it. He would sometimes scratch his head while he said these lines and sit down at the kitchen table and stare at the apple tree he had hated from the first day we moved in.

Racism was present at Firestone, just as it was throughout the town. Akron's Summit Ku Klux Klan was extremely active at one time, the membership including public officials and members of the school board. The rubber factories were founded on racism. The

Liberian worker on the cover of the Firestone pamphlet my dad brought home was a perfect symbol for the company. Black—and Appalachian—workers made the whole industry possible. Black migration from the South began to grow in 1920, as the rubber industry grew. In 1910 there were 657 blacks in all of Akron. By 1920, the number had increased to 5,580. Ten years later, that figure had more than doubled. The war expanded the need for jobs, and 12,000 more blacks found their way to Rubber Town in the 1940s. During the Great Depression, though, blacks in Akron were laid off at twice the rate whites were. Throughout the 1950s there were no white collar jobs in the rubber industry for blacks. It would be 1956 before the city would employ its first black bus driver.

My dad breathed in Firestone's message every day, the same way he had breathed in lampblack. But suddenly he began to feel what it really meant to be black—discredited by managers, placed on a dock to load tires too heavy for any man, covered with dirt all the time.

This shouldn't be happening to him, he may have reasoned, because he was *not* black. But it *was* happening. So it must be happening for some other reason than the color of my father's skin. The company had given him a dirty job he hated, lowered his pay, stripped him of his ambition to be a leader in his plant, and then stopped talking to him. Like all of us in the 1960s, but for his own reasons, and in his own way, I think my father began to think. To *really* use his brain.

Before the 1960s, it may have never crossed Tom Coyne's mind that blacks might not *like* the jobs they had been given in the factories, nor many of the other jobs that let them survive in Akron, Ohio. During his long series of demotions throughout the 1960s and the 1970s, I think it dawned on my father that he had something in common with *his coloreds* that had nothing at all to do with skin.

It was about this time I noticed that my dad began to learn the

last names of black workers at his plant, though I realize only now
what this might have meant.

✎✎

I'm able to see something else that terrifies me.

Just days after Firestone fired him, I received a call from my
mother, asking my husband and me to drive down to the Park. I did-
n't know then that Tom Coyne had been fired, or when it had occurred, so I didn't see a connection between her summons and what
Firestone had just done to my dad.

"He's siphoned antifreeze right into his stomach," Mother said,
as calmly as she could, considering what she was telling me. I sometimes don't know if my mother was just calm by nature, or if she got
that way from living with Thomas Coyne.

"Call an ambulance!" I said.

"You know Dad," she said.

"Please!"

"Just come," she said. She hung up.

We did what she asked us to. We drove the familiar fifteen miles
from our home to Firestone Park. Faster than we ever had before.

There on the sofa was my dad, almost green. He had just wanted
to drain the radiator, he said. But he had chosen the darkest hour of
the evening to do it, with only a flashlight balanced on the edge of
the car for light. He'd always prided himself on his skill as a mechanic, on how the gas stations in town had bid for his services when he
was a young man. The story of how he stripped a car to its chassis
and built it back up—all alone—was one of his favorites.

But here he was, Tom Coyne the mechanic, doing something like
this.

He'd used his own mouth, his own inhaling, to start the fluid's
flow. Too slow, he'd choked and sucked in antifreeze.

"Don't call an ambulance!" he screamed at us. "Let me die right here."

We waited until he stopped groaning and started to snore. I kept one hand on the telephone the whole time. Toward midnight he seemed out of danger, so we left, still not knowing what to say.

"He's a big, stubborn Irishman," my mother finally said as we fumbled with our car keys. She'd said that about W. T. many times, and now that he was dead she was saying it about his son. It was strange to hear these words aimed in Dad's direction, because my mother so seldom said anything that would graze his skin.

I wonder, now, too late to help anyone, if my father was *really* trying to drain the radiator that night the way he said he was. Or had he tried to take his life?

Did he hope my mother wouldn't find him outside at that hour, with that tube stuck deep down into the radiator? Had he planned to drink more of the fluid than he did, but my mother called to him through the screen of the bathroom window before his drink was through, startling him back to life? Had he just wanted to die in his backyard by the birdbath and the apple tree, die on the ground of his Evergreen Avenue property? I didn't suspect any of this the night I answered my mother's call.

"Just getting old," I said to my husband as we rode home, finding a simple way to explain this thing my dad had done. A way that *we* could understand.

People didn't drink antifreeze in Firestone Park and kill themselves. When my husband and I drove home that night the thought never entered our conscious minds that my father may have lost something so important to him that he wasn't sure he wanted to live without it. Self-pride, a place to be, a desk to dust, a destination to drive to every single morning for all those years—it was all gone. Tom Coyne had lost the Firestone Tire & Rubber Company.

If your lover leaves you, let's say, rejects you after thirty-seven years, wouldn't you know the kind of darkness I think my father saw the night he opened his car hood and stared down into the engine at the cap on his radiator? Firestone was no less than his lover all that time. I think it was more.

He may have felt so bad that for one brief moment—at least for one gulp on that plastic hose—he very much wanted never to wake up again in that little Tudor house that sat on the edge of a street shaped like a crescent moon.

CHAPTER 15

❦❦❦

My father might have tried to leave the world *again,* but he made a discovery that kept him here. This was the story stored in my father's URW folder, the middle scenes of the final act.

Something gave him hope shortly after that cold, dark night in 1972 that still haunts me.

Tom Coyne found his old union contract.

Because he had begun his career with the union, my father was legally permitted to reclaim his clock card number—#9786. That was his discovery. So he became a union man once more, a laborer. He was just *laid off* now, not *fired,* he could tell people a little more proudly. He sat at home restlessly waiting for a labor job to open up, for the day the phone would ring and the voice on the other end would offer him a job—as a janitor.

While he waited, he applied to serve as a member of the staff of District 1 of the URW on Massillon Road. He received a letter of acceptance from URW International President Peter Bommarito on May 4, 1971, a letter addressed to Brother Coyne and signed "Fraternally yours, P. Bommarito." If he couldn't be plant manager, my dad decided he could at least use the union to warn his friends. If he couldn't receive a letter from Harvey Firestone, he could at least be sent one from the union president who fought the company he'd loved.

Even while my father was alive, I knew in a sort of vague way that he was working for the union, but I never understood why, and I was too naïve about company policy then to suspect that joining the union had anything to do with being fired by Firestone. The only thing I really understood was that my dad was happier now, and more fun to be around. I joked and called him the Plant Prophet, but he didn't smile the way I thought he would when I said it.

Now I know why. This was serious business to Tom Coyne, not the Joke of the Day.

His union leaders, the few who are still alive, have told me that Tom Coyne organized salaried personnel, what the union called the Firestone Salary Group. He organized people who were just like *he* used to be. He told them the wrecking ball was on its way, heading right toward them, and they better get ready—join the union. They were not safe, he said. They were not *set for life* the way they thought they had been.

I had always felt that my dad's phrase *set for life* was a little like the *Amen* on the Lord's Prayer. It was final. After you heard it, you could take a deep breath. Dad always took a huge gulp of air as soon as the words were out.

I heard him say *set for life* the day we moved to Firestone Park. "We're set for life now, Annabelle!" he said, bobbing his head and pressing his lips together.

But now my dad knew the whole structure that once was Firestone would soon come tumbling down *and all the king's horses, and all the king's men, couldn't put Firestone together again.* He must have stared out the windows of the plant in those final days and seen the wrecking ball in the distance, first a shadow, then a shape, coming closer and closer to everyone's head—and heard its awful swoosh.

Tom Coyne knew now that just because a man was on salary

didn't make him safe. It was a simple message, and perhaps a simple truth, but to Tom Coyne it was a revelation, something it had taken him all his life to understand. He had to deliver his message to men in the other plants, and to do it he would use all of the speaking skills he had acquired in his Firestone classrooms.

My dad would never sign another business letter without his clock number underneath his name. I wonder, sometimes, if I should have had the stonecutter at Holy Cross Cemetery carve *Clock #9786* on his tombstone under his dates of birth and death. I think Tom Coyne might have liked that.

A labor leader who now lives in Florida told me my dad's work with the union was a disaster. Tom Coyne couldn't convince people who had office jobs and wore clean, white shirts that the company would ever strike them down—or raze their factories. He couldn't bring the issue to a vote because not enough salaried employees would sign cards asking for union representation, and that had to come first.

So Tom Coyne stopped working for the union and returned to his sofa, propped his head up with one hand and waited for the phone to ring.

It finally did.

Working as a janitor—all the lifting, pushing, bending that was involved—caused my dad's intestines to break open again, and bleed. The doctors at Firestone who examined him before he returned to work said he could do the job. I found the details of that medical exam in his folder. But I was with him on the trips to the Cleveland Clinic he took just a few months after he started that new job (though I didn't know why he was having all this trouble again), and doctors there insisted that if he didn't stop straining his abdomen he would die. I didn't know that was code between doctors

and Mr. Coyne for *stop lifting tires and pushing brooms.* I thought
Dad just had to promise not to mow the grass anymore, and he'd be
fine.

He trusted the clinic by now far more than he did the company,
so he retired in August of 1973. And then he lived seventeen more
years.

The same summer he left Firestone, a wrecking ball supported
on a huge crane delivered the final blow to the beams of Xylos, and
my father's plant crashed to the ground. A huge black cloud lifted
into the air, drifted over other factories in the complex, then disappeared in the prevailing wind. Dust settled on our roof. We had to
close the windows to keep Xylos out.

☙❧

Steve Love and David Giffels, Akron journalists who wrote the
story of the Akron rubber industry, talk about the complex reasons
rubber failed in our town. Among the *many* they explore were the
triennial strikes of unions throughout the 1960s and 1970s, along
with union work rules and issues of wages and benefits. I know
they're right. I know the unions were not perfect and were in part to
blame for rubber leaving town. But what I know even more certainly
is that despite its many faults and weaknesses, the union saved my
father from despair. When Tom Coyne became a union organizer,
his heart grew ten times its normal size, his vision cleared, and for
the first time in his life he saw Firestone as it really was. He saw other things, too.

As the wrecking ball came closer, Tom Coyne shouted out a
warning. *Don't be fooled,* he told salaried personnel from the union
hall. And then he came home and said the words to me.

Don't be fooled, dear Ann, he told me a hundred times before he
died.

And The Walls Come A-Tumbling Down

Xylos being destroyed by the wrecking ball (Courtesy of Bridgestone/Firestone, Inc.)

I had no idea what he meant, or that he was a union organizer, or what he was even talking about. He never told me *who* would fool me, or *why*. What did he mean? I had a college degree and was on my way to graduate school and I was the daughter of Tom and Annabelle Coyne who loved me more than any daughter ever deserved to be loved. Who would want to hurt *me?* Who would ever want to make a fool of me when all I ever did was work hard and get good grades and stay out of trouble and try to be nice to people most of the time?

My father could warn, *Don't be fooled,* he could say it to me every time I walked into the living room of his Evergreen Avenue house (which he pretty much did around this time), but the love I felt from him contradicted the very words he spoke. His love was free of all deceit and I heard, instead, *this is not for you, my dear, no, not for you to worry about.* He was only an old man who had fallen prey to doubt and fear, even older things than he was.

I refused to smell the ground with my nose the way he did now, looking for signs of blood. With his Richard Nixon jowls, *he* was the great bloodhound, not me. The skin was high and tight on *my* cheekbones, and no one would ever guess that my body sometimes fluttered just the way my father's did. Even I ignored this link to him.

I was no more attentive to my father's voice than I was to the whir of his Norelco shaver.

CHAPTER 16

Tom Coyne refused to mention the name of his company for fifteen years after the wrecking ball took his building down.

We both read the *Akron Beacon Journal* every day, and knew a little bit about what was going on at Firestone, but we didn't talk about it the way we had before—each blip on the company screen a heartbeat in our own chests.

Sometimes I'd see him shake his head when he'd see a story about yet another Firestone factory being razed in Akron. His white hair would shoot in long strands toward his nose. What had happened to us, and to Xylos, would be repeated many times before the Firestone story was over.

Plant 2 closed in 1978. A wrecking crew battled its steel and concrete for two years before the building finally fell, a winter sacrifice.

I could tell the news about other closings upset my dad, because the burps started up for a few days each time it happened. He probably was thinking of all the men who would lose their jobs. Of the workers who would fill out unemployment forms, file for divorce, leave town, take out loans to go to barber school. A few really *would* commit suicide.

The rubber industry had changed in so many ways that men like my father no longer recognized it, and the industry no longer recognized them. Thirty-one tire plants were built in the United States between 1960 and 1979, and twenty-four of those were in the South

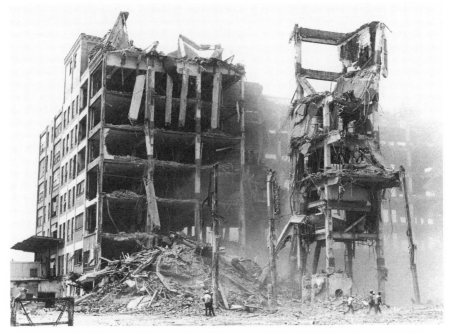

Firestone Plant 2, demolition, 1979 (© Daniel Mainzer)

where the URW's constant demands for salaries to keep up with exorbitant inflation rates could be ignored. Akron's old plants, like Xylos, were seldom modernized or equipped with radial-tire technology—the way of the future for the tire industry.

Over and over we watched the factories turn into empty buildings, the bricks and windows grow darker and more bleak. Finally, we saw them collapse and disappear. A few were converted into offices or warehouses: The machinery of production gave way to desks and little shelves, and the sounds inside grew light. They were hives with insects in them now, not hot slaughterhouses with roaming beasts.

The closings upset me too, though in a selfish way. I would miss Plant 2. It stood directly behind our house, on the other side of South Main. That old plant was the background I grew up against. You could almost draw a straight line from my backyard to the statue of Harvey Firestone and then to Plant 2. The building had always seemed as old and permanent to me as the arrowheads I found buried in Aunt Lil's yard on the edge of her lake.

On the roof of that plant was a large red neon sign that said *Firestone,* just like the sign on the roof of Plant 1 at the entrance to Firestone Parkway and the factory complex. It lit up the sky—when Akron air was clear enough to see the sky—and its glow flowed right in our bathroom window. It was the nightlight of my youth.

I used to wait until my parents fell asleep and then walk across the narrow hall to the tiny bathroom, pull aside the white curtain on the window, and bathe in the light of the luminous letters that spelled the name of my father's company.

Then I would sneak from the bathroom to the little powder room next to it where my mother dressed for work, spray my wrists with cologne—the way I saw my mother do—press lipstick on my lips, then a dab on each cheek, like rouge, and rub it in. I would crawl back into bed, kiss the palm of my hand, and smell myself turning into a woman.

I kept the bathroom door and my bedroom door wide open so that some of the red light from the sign always spilled onto my pillow and mixed with the glow of the streetlight. The light that ushered in my dreams didn't come from stars, but from Firestone.

As I lay there, soaked in neon red, I could see the boy next door through my window. His bedroom was right across from mine, right above the little privet hedge that formed a wall between our houses. But there were no walls on the bedroom level—no walls in the sky—

*Firestone Plant 2, showing red neon sign, at closing,
1978 (Courtesy of the* Akron Beacon Journal)

so I could watch the handsome boy pace inside. I would sometimes
close my eyes then and dream about the man I would love forever,
and who would love me, and give him names (often "Roger," the
name I gave my dolls) and dress him in different clothes—bathing
suits, tuxedos, pants from dancing school with sequins down the
sides.

Right off my neighbor's room was a tiny balcony, and sometimes, when he grew a little older, and I did too, on warm nights he'd walk out without a shirt and I would see him there. On those nights I wouldn't close my eyes and make things up. A rail hit him below the waist, and as he leaned my way in the red light, I watched the bottom of his pajamas slide softly over his hipbone, and loved the way his flesh curved in.

When that sign fell, it was as if my youth had been canceled out, and the boy had only been a ghost.

Shortly after Plant 2 closed, John Nevin came to town. An executive at Ford Motor Company and chairman of Zenith, he arrived in Akron in 1979 as the company's new president. He intended to clean house, to rescue Firestone from over a billion dollar debt.

The papers kept reporting that profits were up under Nevin's management. In 1980 the *Wall Street Journal* said that the Firestone Tire & Rubber Company *had finally turned around.*

Less than two years after his arrival, Nevin recommended that *seven* of Firestone's seventeen plants be closed, including Plant 1 and Firestone's Seiberling Tire & Rubber Company plant in Barberton, Ohio. Both shut down in 1980. My father read about the closings and sadly bobbed his head.

In 1988, fifteen years after Xylos was razed and my father retired, Tom Coyne broke his vow of silence.

On St. Patrick's Day of that year, Nevin finalized a deal to sell the Firestone Tire & Rubber Company for $2.6 billion dollars to Bridgestone Corporation, Japan's largest tire maker. The company would soon change its name to Bridgestone/Firestone. Nevin retired in December of 1989, having made at least twenty million dollars for himself, much of which he used to buy a controlling interest in Budget Rent a Car Corporation of Chicago.

Before long, Bridgestone/Firestone would move its corporate offices to Nashville, Tennessee, taking only three dates in my father's life along with them. Rubber would virtually disappear from town.

My father talked about the sale with me, and used the name of Firestone for the first time in fifteen years.

"Firestone sold to the Japanese for $80 a share. Can you beat that!" he said.

He had inherited several hundred shares from his father—never sold them—and Tom Coyne now had what he called *a little nest egg*. The trading value had been $7 a share when John Nevin arrived in Akron.

Of course there was pleasure in my father's voice when he talked about the sale. He would have enough money now to take a car trip with my mother through Canada and then back across the whole United States. They'd be able to see practically all the Northern hemisphere, he bragged. Imagine that.

But there was revenge and anger in his voice too.

What I heard when he spoke about the sale of Firestone and his Firestone stock was more like what you'd hear in the voice of a plaintiff who just received a settlement for some damage that can never really be undone. Payment for an arm that was lost, let's say, or a blackened lung, or a child who was scarred forever by some terrible accident.

❧❧

I can't help seeing a connection between the harm that came to my dad and the harm that people in the recall of 2000 have suffered.

Workers lost their jobs in the recall, just the way my father did. In June of 2001 Bridgestone/Firestone announced that it would close its plant in Decatur, Illinois—the plant where most of the tires in the initial recall were manufactured during a period of strikes and replacement hires in the 1990s. During periods of unrest, management in that plant had frequently run the machines, but workers who often hadn't even touched those faulty ATX, ATX II, and Wilderness AT tires were the ones who were forced to leave.

Even worse, customers were harmed or killed by Firestone's carelessness. Tread peeled right off the rims of wheels like black banana skins, and people died or lost their limbs.

It's true that rubber didn't take my father's life the violent way it took the lives of recent victims who died on highways riding on *the name that's known is Firestone, Where the rubber meets the road.*

I can't imagine the horror of such a sudden loss.

With my dad it happened much more slowly. It began in his bowels, then worked its way up—broke his heart, then ate his lungs.

So, in a way, when I heard about all those accidents, all those deaths, I pitied myself too, even as I pitied the recent dead, and all the people left behind to mourn them.

Rubber kills fast sometimes, and sometimes it kills slow.

I knew what it felt like to lose someone to rubber, and as selfish as I know it was, that's the memory the Firestone recall brought back to me. And if I tell the whole truth, in the late hours of the night the recall also made me think about my *own* fate, and still does. In a very real way the air my father breathed was the air *I* breathed too. It was the air of my father's plant—toxic and dark—that traveled in the wind up the hill to the homes in Firestone Park. The same air that gives me stories about life in Rubber Town, and helps me write, filled my pink lungs when I was a girl.

But unlike the stories I put into words and then onto paper, there's no way I can get it out.

And Then Tom Coyne Hunkered Down and Began to Die . . .

❧❧

By the time of the Rededication, I had started to become a little more suspicious of the world. At least, I thought I had.

I recognized the pomp and arrogance of the light show, understood in the official greetings of the mayor and a congressman from the fourteenth district how politics and industry were linked, felt the tension between the Japanese and American branches of the new Firestone family by the way they sat far from one another in the audience and never spoke.

I knew other things, too. I'd just found out from Akron architectural historian Jim Paulau that our little Tudor house, the house Dad always said was one-of-a-kind and built for executives, was a catalog house, assembled from millwork and wood shipped to town by Sears Roebuck. Sears had opened a Modern Homes office in Akron in 1919 (the year our house was built), a probable connection to the decision by Firestone's site superintendent, John F. Suppes, and the Shannon Construction Company to use ready-cut kits and Sears materials.

But the most obvious thing that night escaped me. Firestone was covering up a tragedy that would lead to a massive recall in the next few days. Right there, in the middle of a big party, our host was fooling us, and I was taken in.

Why didn't I notice tension in the posture of Masatoshi Ono when he delivered his remarks, or see the noose around his neck that would soon end his life as the company's CEO? Why didn't I guess from the folded napkins and the complimentary pins and the new repairs of the statue and the lights and the brickwork around the monument that too much energy was being expended on how things looked? How did I miss the discomfort that must have been on the faces of executives? Who knew? Who didn't? Who winced as the well-rehearsed script was read onstage?

Why didn't I take my Swiss army knife and scratch the surface of the statue—right then and there? Why didn't I remember that the noses and toes of the figures on the exedra had been hammered and chiseled off by vandals, an early sign of Harvey's fall from grace? How had I forgotten that "I love Jenn" had once been smeared on Firestone's lapel and "Jake" had been scrawled across his forehead?

Why have I never been an oracle?

How had I missed the sound of my father's voice on a night his spirit surely roamed beside me, restless and afraid? Why were my ears still not ready to hear his words in the August wind, the very month of his death ten short years before?

Don't be fooled. *My father, clear from the dead, would have strained to push his cold breath into the breeze that cut the air, to press his disembodied voice into some form that would let him speak.*

My father never stopped preaching this lesson, even after the Firestone years, and I know the night of the Rededication he was preaching it still through the memory of his death that came to me.

CHAPTER 17

❧❧❧

The Firestone story, the story of *old* Firestone, that is, before Bridgestone bought it up, didn't end when the company was sold. The story continued to spin out in the lives of its workers, because they were the ones who carried its lessons away with them.

The hard lessons Firestone had taught my father stayed with him to his dying day. That's why I can't stop writing until I follow Tom Coyne to the grave.

I wonder, even as I write about him, if my *own* Firestone story will be finished when my father and I part on the final pages of this book, or only when *I* die. My son, an Akron journalist, has *already* written about rubber, so maybe we'll never be able to stop telling this story until every drop of our family's blood has been buried in Akron cemeteries. Maybe even then the ground we lie in will refuse to be vulcanized, will swell and shake until it opens up.

Don't be fooled. Those are the words that will rush from the hard cracks in the ground where my family tries to rest.

After Brother Coyne retired, he would not be fooled. Not once. Not about Firestone. Not about anything. He saw what was *really* there, after that. Not what the statue or Harvey's streetlights promised.

My father never turned away from another wrecking ball. He never turned away from trouble again.

He became the family member who cleaned up messes that other people made. After divorces, evictions, binges of every sort, my dad stepped in. He was the only person who could stand to look at the debris of someone else's life and sweep it up.

His efforts had a rough and funny edge to them, a little like the time he got in trouble for stacking tires so high that his workers nearly disappeared.

But he got things done.

T. W. Coyne was sometimes a little *too* efficient, especially when it came to death.

≈≈≈

One morning in 1985, the family started calling Tom. They were worried about my mother's sister Helen because she wasn't answering her phone. It was Tom Coyne who got in his car and drove to Helen's home on the edge of Goodyear Heights—a community similar to Firestone Park that F. A. Seiberling built for his Goodyear Tire & Rubber Company employees.

I happened to be visiting my folks when the call came and Dad made his decision to drive to Helen's house. He asked me if I'd mind trailing behind, *just in case.* I was ready to head home anyway, and it was just a little out of the way, so I agreed. I really didn't want to—there was something kind of creepy about all this—but my dad asked for so few favors that of course I followed him. I stayed behind a minute to say goodbye to my mother. People were already noticing that Annabelle was having trouble with her memory, and I wanted to make sure she had marked some dates on her calendar before I left.

By the time I pulled into my aunt's driveway, my father had Aunt Helen in his car.

Something was wrong. I knew it. Something was *really* wrong.

Aunt Helen was in the *back* seat, not the passenger seat up by my dad. But who else was going to climb in front with *him,* I wondered? Why would he make Helen sit in back? *I* was on my way home and

Helen and Steve Skladan

had my own car, so it wasn't a place Dad had saved for me. *Steve*, Aunt Helen's husband, had been dead for nearly twenty years, so he wasn't going to join them. No one else was going to get in.

"What's wrong with Aunt Helen, Dad?" I asked, as I looked through the window and saw her head topple over, and her body slide toward the door.

"Dead," Dad said.

"Dead?!" I screamed, hoping no one heard me, or caught a

glimpse of what was going on right outside their cute little bunga-
lows.

"Died in her sleep. A blessing to go like that."

"But what are you doing with Helen *now?*" I asked.

"Taking her to emergency so they can see she's dead and we can
get things set up at Eckard-Baldwin for the funeral. She is *dead,* you
know."

"Couldn't we call someone to do this *for* us?" I asked.

"Why?" my dad said. "We're here, we have a car, and she's dead,
so why not just do it ourselves? I think she'd rather ride with us than
some guy she doesn't even know who drives an ambulance."

I had no words.

My father insisted he didn't need me any longer. He had thought
something might have been wrong, but *no problem here.* I headed
home, mortified by what had just happened in front of my aunt's
tiny little house, the place where we used to grill steaks in the backyard every Memorial Day.

I was very upset that my aunt had died, of course. Aunt Helen
was a loving soul, and always nice to me. She crocheted afghans and
spent months needlepointing flowers on the seats of her dining-
room chairs.

At the Lutheran church in Goosetown, she was famous for the
stories she wrote about Jesus and love. She was the most famous author I knew for a long time. She and I would sometimes sit in her living room, books on either side of the fireplace and the family Bible
open on the coffee table. (The Evergreen Avenue house only had
one small bookcase that held the *World Book Encyclopedia* we
bought from a salesman who came to the door one winter night and
Dad's Zane Grey and Dale Carnegie collections.) Then we would
write. She would start me out on little essays with titles like "Faith"

and "Home" and "Flags." But I often noticed that Helen spent most of *her* time on an essay she kept in the back of her Bible called "Widowhood." She never showed it to me when we wrote together (she preferred to have me think about things like home as a friendly port and Tony the poor immigrant boy who led a school parade carrying Old Glory), but I found it in my father's papers (he kept hers too, along with the papers of all our dead). Those paragraphs about her terrible loneliness on Sunday afternoons were the only ones that brought her voice back to me.

Although I probably shouldn't admit it, my amazement at what my father had done was even greater than the sadness I was feeling for my poor aunt.

He had gone in the house, found her dead in her bed, removed her nightclothes and dressed her in a blouse and pants (as if she were about to take a morning walk), carried her outside in his arms, locked the door behind him, and laid her body in the back seat of his Chrysler. He'd even put her hat on and pulled down the veil.

I should have known then that Tom Coyne was almost ready for the crane to pull up in his own driveway.

CHAPTER 18

And it did. Shortly after my aunt Helen died.

For a long time my father and I had noticed changes in my mother, though I refused to say the word I knew I needed in order to describe them. I pushed it farther and farther away the closer it came.

But my father knew the word, and *said* it. He said it like a fact.

He always said it wrong—pronouncing it his own way. But he *said* it, and that's what no one else had the courage to do.

"She's got it, all right. Old-zeimer's," he would say when Annabelle did something odd. Before this, the oddest thing I can remember ever seeing my mother do was sew little skirts on a couple of end tables. She was so sane that I sometimes failed to understand her.

But now she was disoriented when she traveled any distance, or just walked into a kitchen other than her own. On one short trip we all took together, my mother stood over my bed in our motel room, early in the morning, and asked me to come and see her new house. I admired the shower stall, the double sink, the heavy curtains with rubber backing, the picture of Elvis on the wall that Annabelle insisted was a portrait of her father, August.

The trip they took on Firestone stock lasted six whole weeks, longer than they'd ever been away from the Park. It was the last trip they made together. The morning after their return, Annabelle stared at my dad across the toast and eggs he had made for her and

Annabelle Coyne and Helen Skladan

said, "Tommy, why don't you take me anywhere anymore?"

"Annabelle," he said, "we—"

"What's happened, Tommy?" she interrupted. "You used to be such a nice man."

Everything seemed to fall apart for my mom after Helen died. Maybe Annabelle realized it was all right to be ill now herself since Helen was gone. Helen couldn't drive and had relied on my mother's car for two solid decades. For the last few years, Helen needed a lot more than just a ride to the Acme. She had gotten "weird" was the way my mother put it, until my mother got so strange herself that she couldn't recognize weird anymore.

Helen put things in all the wrong places (silverware on the book-

shelves, a picture of her dead husband in the refrigerator, her reading glasses Lord-knows-where), seldom cleaned her house, forgot to
throw out old milk and soggy Lipton teabags. She just sat on her
porch all day and stared at the neighbor's truck.

Helen probably would not have been able to stay in her own
house without the visits of Annabelle and her other sisters. Annabelle knew this.

Helen would be the first of the five Haberkost sisters who would
develop Alzheimer's disease. One sister died of breast cancer at fifty-
nine, but the other four lived long lives, and they all died of
Alzheimer's. Helen was the oldest of the sisters, and the first to lose
her mind.

It was impossible not to notice how truly weird Helen had become. My parents would always take Aunt Helen to Sunday brunch
with them, and sometimes I'd join them, though I dreaded it. Helen
consumed food like a furnace, filling her cheeks with great gobs of it.
She often choked, but never seemed to notice anything was wrong.
While Tom Coyne would beat her on the back, Helen would contin-
ue to smile and giggle, completely unaware that her breath had nearly left her.

My mother was the second daughter in her family, born four
years after Helen. So after Helen died, she was next in line.

Annabelle's Alzheimer's was a far more virulent variety than my
aunt Helen's, but my father, unlike *his* father, never told me to take
Annabelle away.

"Get that woman out of here!" I can still hear my grandpa say
about Bessie Coyne. The nursing home where Bessie lived after her
gravy did her in sedated her for ten years, and pretty much forgot
that she was there. Her strong heart kept on beating, so they saved
her a bed, but every time I went to visit her she was all alone,

strapped down in a corner of a dark room so still that dust hung suspended in the air, and never moved.

My grandpa didn't visit Grandma once. Not a single day after she left the Reed Avenue house did he spend with his wife of over fifty years. Not a single second more with *that woman.*

Tom Coyne never visited his mother either. That job fell to my mother, and sometimes to me, when she made me go along (and I hated it). But when it happened a second time, to Annabelle, my father had become *himself,* not his dad anymore, and he never left his wife's side. I sometimes wonder if Bessie and Annabelle ever mixed in his mind, mother and wife becoming one, allowing him to pay the debt he owed, the debt his father owed, through his absolute devotion to Annabelle. To *this woman.*

W. T. frowned and waved his wife away. T. W. dug his heels in, let Annabelle loose, and chased her in the wind.

He cooked for her, even though the only thing he'd ever done in the kitchen before was get in the way. He suddenly turned into a gourmand, and his kitchen became a French café. It looked like a page from a fancy catalog—cookbooks everywhere, waffle irons, Cuisinarts, little pots of herbs on windowsills. My father loved his new role and served banquets every night, with wines and sauces, and basil scissored over everything. Just for the two of them. It was the most romantic period of their entire lives.

He set up routines she could rely on. Breakfast at Bob Evans around ten o'clock, a simple lunch at home, a trip to the mall for exercise early in the afternoon. Around and around they'd walk, and each time they circled, my mother would comment on the same colorful window displays she'd commented on the time before. Then home to a spectacular meal at the Evergreen Café.

Tom Coyne sorted her dirty laundry (when my mother would allow him in her room), then put Annabelle in the car and headed to the laundromat.

He tried to make my mother feel normal, even though *nothing* was normal anymore. He made sure she went to her sixtieth high-school reunion when the invitation arrived in their mailbox. Dad had Mother fitted for a dress—a beautiful beige chiffon with puffy sleeves—and stayed right beside her at the banquet while she tried to talk to her women friends.

"Who *were* those nice people, Tommy?" she said on the way home, the same confusion rising in her voice that he'd heard the morning after Canada.

"Annabelle!" my father snapped, and shook his head.

Everyone would become a stranger to her before this thing was over. Me. My father. Eventually her own reflection in a mirror.

Dad was irritated sometimes. He was not a saint. Mother would keep opening the windows and the doors in summertime. She had forgotten her house had air conditioning. She had forgotten what air conditioning even was, because she was a young girl now, and it hadn't been invented yet. On hot days, my father prayed she'd slow down a little and fall asleep in a rocking chair.

"Stop it now, Annabelle!" I would sometimes hear him yell when I drove in the driveway to visit.

But he seemed to sleep off every annoyance with this strange creature he shared his Firestone Park house with now. He would get up each morning to the alarm on his Firestone radio and for one more day try to keep the world together for Annabelle. And for himself. And, I know now, for me.

She became violent, and sometimes screamed at Tom Coyne or punched him in the stomach, or slapped his face. But he just stood there, tears welling up in his eyes. He folded his arms and shook his great head. I noticed the lines on his forehead growing deeper, and his jowls growing longer.

"Ah, Annabelle, Annabelle, *please* Annabelle," he would say, pleading with her for something he couldn't name.

My mother wouldn't bathe, so he washed her. At night she would put her hearing aids in the Efferdent solution. In the morning my dad would have to write another pleading letter to the insurance company asking for replacements.

She would refuse to step inside the beauty shop she had gone to for thirty years, so my father learned to brush and curl her golden hair. One day I arrived and he was wrapping endpapers around huge strands and holding her head gently with both hands, trying to dip it into neutralizer.

My parents were nearly forty when I was born, so they always seemed old. And unromantic. I just knew they *never* could have felt the streak of heat *I* felt up and down the inside of my thighs when boys came near. They seldom laughed. Sometimes they talked about a dance at Summit Beach, but I found it hard to imagine them whirling under a mirrored chandelier in each other's arms. They were *old,* never young, to me.

I had no idea what I was looking at. Now I know I'll never see anything like it again. Not anywhere. Not in all the world. The way my father loved my mother in the throes of her disease—the way he *always* loved her—was spectacular.

I should have known before my mother grew so ill that my parents had this love. I should have seen it in the patience my mother always had with my father. He annoyed her—he annoyed a lot of people—but she seldom would complain.

Once, when I made fun of my father's weight, my mother grew very stern—not a word I often think of when I think of her. I'll never

Annabelle and T. W. Coyne, the Alzheimer's years

forget her response, because it was so rare. She treated me, almost always, as if I were both in her house and absent from it. Hers was an aloof love. She watched me—when there was time—with interest and curiosity, but without any clear intention or purpose for my life. I adored her even then for the independence her unconventional maternity provided me.

My father had been gaining weight and I'd called him "Biggy," then doubled over and laughed my cackly adolescent laugh.

Even Tom Coyne sort of chuckled when he heard the name, but my mother rushed me to another room.

"Never say that again," she said. "Your father works harder than any man alive, and he loves you more than you'll ever know. Why can't you see that?"

And then I watched her turn her attention from me and begin to think about what she had said—think about why something so obvious to *her* remained hidden from *me*. I was her daughter and had her hair, her eyes, her long neck, and yet there was this basic difference between us that she couldn't account for. Her powdered blue eyes rolled off my face like a piece of sky and looped in a new direction, and it was over, just like that.

My mother knew something because her father was August Haberkost and left them all whenever heat was in the summer air and the smell of the brewery grew strong. And this is what she knew: Tom Coyne would never leave her. Nor would he ever *want* to leave, not for a single instant in their long marriage. And he would never leave the daughter that they'd had, no matter what, no matter how many terrible things I said to him. That's why I couldn't say them anymore.

But what I don't know is if she ever imagined the dimension of this man's loyalty to her. Even when the woman that he loved completely disappeared, and a stranger arrived to take her place, he would stay and love what was left. She belonged to him, even when nothing except the smell of her remained, the raw, strong smell of the only woman that he'd ever loved.

CHAPTER 19

The air in my father's lungs was made of tar from Camel cigarettes, lampblack from the Xylos plant, and the waste of rubber that
pushed up smokestacks on its way to our homes. I thought all air
was dark when I was young. Thick, black Akron air was more real to
me than oxygen you couldn't even see.

Sour smoke floated from west to east in the prevailing winds,
right up our hill into the windows of our little Tudor house.

You had it with your coffee in the morning, and your meat loaf at
night.

Seasons had no odors in Firestone Park. Even in early spring, the
smell of the lilac bush at the side of our house was not strong enough
to perfume the air or float through screen doors, the way lilacs did in
other towns.

We scraped rubber from our windowpanes with razor blades,
like rime.

The final wrecking ball that crashed through the walls of our
Evergreen Avenue house ended my father's life. It swung through
the window of his Tudor house—like the pendulum on some great
clock—picked him up, and shot him loose into the universe.
Launched him like a giant rubber band.

He had been having trouble breathing, and was coughing all the
time now, but he refused to leave my sick mother long enough to see

Annabelle and T. W. Coyne, just before his fatal illness

a doctor about his *own* ill health. *Her* Alzheimer's had become my father's full-time job, and he never missed a day.

I finally put him in the car with me—he in the passenger seat, my mother in the back asking over and over where I was taking her, and pulling my hair.

"Hey, you! What's this all about?"

We drove to the emergency room of Akron City Hospital, the hospital where most people in our family are born, then go to die. Nurses hooked my father up to oxygen and wheeled him into a room when they saw the way he was struggling for breath. My mother and I sat and waited.

It was like taking care of a child now, when I waited anywhere with my mom. She grew restless right away without Tom Coyne by her side. She tired of magazines and started to pluck the cords of her neck like strings on the violin she once played, maybe wishing she could have it back. Have everything back. *Anything* back. Then her fingers moved to her face and she dug red ridges into her cheeks with her thick nails.

Four long hours later, a staff doctor came out to tell me they had found a mass in my father's lung.

He had a vicious form of lung cancer. "Environmentally induced," the doctor said. The air he had breathed all those years in the factory, and in the Park, was now about to kill him.

When I heard the diagnosis, I thought about him smoking on breaks at work. And about the Camels always resting in our house on tables, counters, the TV top—small pieces of tobacco everywhere, as common as dust. And about how proud he'd been of finally quitting his habit. It was one of the proudest feats of his adult life (*I quit April 10, 1965,* he'd say whenever he found an opening in a conversation). But he had not quit soon enough.

I thought about the chemicals he'd breathed, and the dirty job of reclaim that was his great delight for so long.

My father was admitted to the hospital, and early the next day we all gathered around his bed, waiting for Tom Coyne's family doctor to arrive. My cousin—"Dr. Paul," my dad called him, out of deep respect for doctors and the education that they had—stopped his rounds at Akron City Hospital and leaned on an aluminum rail over Tom Coyne, dangling his stethoscope like a pendant on a silver chain.

When Dad's doctor came in, my cousin drew back.

"What do you want to know, Coyne?" the doctor asked, staring directly at him. He addressed him the way he always had, the way my father wanted to be addressed at the factory—a little rough. But the strange part was that while the doctor spoke, he cupped my father's hand and stroked it with the largest, softest thumb I'd ever seen.

"All of it," Tom Coyne said, point blank, his thick lips quivering.

"Six weeks," the doctor said. "There's no doubt you're going to meet your maker this time, Coyne."

᯽᯽᯽

That same doctor—he'd taken care of Mr. Coyne for over twenty years—used to tell me my dad was as strong as a great oak, *strong as a tree, your father,* he'd say. But he didn't say it to me around my father's hospital bed, and I knew he would never say it again. I heard its absence more clearly than I heard the details he gave about my father's lung.

All the loss of the American Elms in my neighborhood when I was a girl came back to me in his silence, and I knew what happened to the trees in the Park was only the smallest hint of the grief that lay just six weeks ahead of me. Six weeks ahead of my dad. Six weeks, *six of the best, six-shooter, six of one and half a dozen of the other, at sixes and sevens, sixty-four-thousand-dollar question, six feet tall.*

Six feet below the ground.

The doctor explained how they would go into my father's chest and drain one lung. "You'll be more comfortable, Coyne," he said.

He told him how they would hook my father up to oxygen around the clock. And how it would finally be his old heart that would just give out trying to run on so little air. And it would probably happen in the middle of the night, when he was asleep, and he would never even know.

My father sat there and asked questions, just the way he might have on a visit to the reclaim plant at Pequanoc Rubber in Pennsylvania to get ideas for improving his plant. He may as well have been asking about mill rolls, grinders, mesh screens, sludge, magnets on conveyor systems, Sargent dryers, scrap storage bins, fumes and leaks from devulcanizers.

He wanted to know about medications and morphine, inhaling through an oxygen mask, the procedure that would drain his lung. This thing was going to happen to him, and he wasn't going to pretend it was not. He would not let the doctor fool him. Nor would he let Death.

He wouldn't let Death take him, just like that, at midnight. He would confront Him, and he would find his huge voice one more time and speak to Death, even though his lungs were all destroyed.

"Hello, Death," he would say. "I'll go with you today, Sir, but you're no friend of mine."

They would leave together, two skeletons instead of one, but my father would refuse to link his arm with Death at the elbow joint.

"What will it feel like, Doc?" he whispered after all the answers had been given. "What will Death feel like when He comes for me?"

❦❦❦

Shortly after Tom Coyne got this news in his hospital room, a slender black minister dressed in a summer suit came to visit the patient next to him, a member of his congregation. His Bible bulging under his arm like an extra muscle, the minister saw my dad sitting in a chair, holding his forehead in his hands. The man was on his way out, but he stopped to talk to my father.

"Are you in distress, Brother?" he asked.

"I'm going to die," my father said.

"Are you in pain, Sir?"

"In pain," my father said.

"Do you want me to pray with you?" the minister said.

"I can use all the help I can get, Reverend," my father answered.

"Heal this poor man, sweet Jesus, heal your son—" he began, then paused. "What's your name, Friend?"

My father told him and the man started up again. "Heal Mr. Coyne, sweet Jesus! Give him peace. Take his pain away, and carry the cross for him over this rough water, Jesus. Sweet Jesus, see him here lying on this bed of nails and remember your child. Remember Mr. Coyne."

Then the minister removed his hand from his chest—it was resting just above his heart—and placed it on my dad's forehead. He prayed with him until the hour was up. The words he spoke floated into the air, but the touch of the man's skin pressed into the flesh of Mr. Coyne, and stuck.

"Amen," he said at last, and finally took his hand away.

The man left with a woman in a teal dress who had accompanied him, but not before he wrote down a phone number for my father.

"When it gets hard, you call me, Sir," he said, folding the paper and sliding it next to my father's water glass.

I don't know if Tom Coyne ever made that call. But I sometimes would see him touch his forehead where the man in the pinstriped suit had placed his palm. He seemed to block the whole world out when he did this, or press the whole world in. It was impossible to tell which it was. I saw him repeat the gesture off and on the rest of his days on earth.

Those days indeed were numbered, and added up to about six weeks. Just what the doctor ordered.

෨෨෨

So we removed all the clocks.

One of the first things my father did after the ambulance brought him home to die was order me to carry all the clocks out of the living room. He wanted them stopped, then taken upstairs where he would not have to look at them or hear them tick the remaining hours of his life away.

He concentrated all his effort on the hospital bed we rented (he refused to let us buy one, *not a good investment,* he said), his portable toilet with silver handrails, and the long cord that fed oxygen into his nose from a tank that stood like a green bomb in the corner of his room. It was not the face of the clock he looked at in these difficult days, but the gauge on that metal tank. Life was measured for him in molecules of oxygen now, not hours or minutes in a day. Not months and decades anymore. And if the long cord twisted or creased, he screamed for help. If no one came, he howled.

He was too ill to take care of Annabelle, so my mother came to live with us.

And then Tom Coyne hunkered down and began to die.

He was absolutely terrified, the way I expect I'll be when my death sentence is delivered. I came to hate that oxygen tank, the toilet, the cord that caused my father's heart to beat too fast and sweat to rush down the deep lines of his face, digging to the bone.

But courage has nothing to do with not being afraid. It has to do with something else my father had. He chose to live the rest of his life knowing he would die. He talked about Death all the time, and shook, and gnashed his teeth. He refused to fool himself.

And he certainly refused to let anyone *else* fool him.

"You're looking at a dead man," he said when visitors tried to cheer him up, tried to tell him how good he looked. People stopped knocking at the door because my father allowed no lies inside his house anymore. Neighbors left an occasional cake, some Jell-O, then quickly backed away and disappeared down the street.

All the blinds on Evergreen were drawn, except for ours.

Don't be fooled was the warning he lived by even when Death was so close I could smell his breath in the living room. Tom Coyne refused to run, and he refused to hide. I saw Mr. Coyne shortly after Death came for him. I'd never seen a dead man, but there my father was lying on his back. His eyes were opened wide. They were full of terror, and I never will forget them. I had to leave the room and ask my father's nurse to press them closed.

He *saw* Death, exactly what he vowed to do. There's no doubt of that.

But Mr. Coyne didn't leave with Death until he taught us one more lesson. There was one more thing to do before he'd open up the door and let Death walk inside.

♥♥♥

My son had just graduated from high school, and was helping me almost every day with the care of my father. Often the three of us—my husband, my son, and I—alternated shifts. My husband would visit in the morning, Stephen in the afternoon, and I would drive to Evergreen Avenue in the evening and hold my father's hand until he fell asleep at night. He was always most afraid at night.

For some reason I completely forget, one day, about a week before my father died, my son and I drove to Firestone Park together.

*Daniel Osborn Dyer and Stephen Osborn Dyer at high-school
graduation, 1990*

Watchcase vulcanizers (Courtesy of Bridgestone/Firestone, Inc.)

Tom Coyne was sitting in the middle of the living room on his plastic toilet, the seat down, his arms draped over the aluminum rails, the nurse shaping a mitt with her washcloth to begin his bath.

As I saw him hanging there, I thought about his first job with Firestone as a watchcase vulcanizer. That's the title he had then. The watchcase, shaped like a pocket watch, was a giant machine where tires were cured—*vulcanized* so they wouldn't melt in the summer and crack in the winter. Tom Coyne had been Vulcan himself in the 1930s—a strong man who stood all day at a forge.

He could not even squeeze his own fingers now, let alone press a tire into resilient life, and cure it.

The nurse was just about to wash his face when Tom Coyne saw us come in the front door, brushed her hand away, and told her to go into another room. His manner was extremely brusque, but hospice nurses are used to this, and she quickly disappeared. He was, after all, a dying man, and few requests would go ungranted.

Then my father told my son to unsnap his pajama bottoms for him and help him lower them. Stephen was startled. He had never seen his grandpa naked, and the request was so unusual that my son froze. Finally, though, he unsnapped his grandpa's cotton pants and helped him slide them down his legs.

Next, Tom Coyne told Stephen to go to the kitchen and dip into warm water the washcloth the nurse had left, and soap it up. My son obeyed.

When Stephen returned to the living room with a cloth full of lather, Dad grabbed his wrist and placed his grandson's hand on his genitals.

"Wash me," he said.

My son, so young, his own adolescent body still changing dramatically, was horrified. And so was I. I tried to help Stephen. I had never seen my father's penis before, except an occasional glimpse as a child when he scooted down the hall from the bathroom with his towel carelessly knotted around his waist. It was enormous, and he was uncircumcised. I had never known. The whole scene was unreal to me. My son and I fumbled together, washing this man's most private parts.

I finally called the nurse to finish, because I couldn't bear the humiliation I was feeling—for my dad, for myself, for my son beside me. I was repulsed by my father's request. I thought for a brief instant that he had lost his mind. The drugs had been responsible for this. All the morphine he was taking. I didn't understand what was really happening here, and neither did Stephen, but I knew I wanted it to stop.

After we wiped my dad as best we could, and just before the nurse arrived from the other room, my father spoke.

He bent toward me, and then toward my son. "Thank you," he said. "One day you'll have to do that."

This line only confused me more. Certainly my father had the tense wrong here. *He* needed help *now,* with *his* bath, so why was he suggesting that this was something we should remember for another time?

Of course what I have come to understand is that my father was showing me what it would take to care for Annabelle Coyne, once he left me alone with her. And he was showing Stephen what it would take to care for me someday when I, too, would grow weak and old. And that day would come. It *will* come. He was showing me how to love my mother, and his grandson how to love his daughter. He had probably bathed Annabelle a thousand times this way since Alzheimer's had left her helpless. It was just something he did, and we would have to do it too.

Brother Coyne was teaching us about love and the old heart. He was vulcanizing still, as he had in the old days, making us stronger through the sulfur and heat of his lessons.

We were standing at T. W.'s fiery forge.

When the fireworks were over, the world lost its color again. A few white lights were all that lit Harvey's face now. People hurried to the parking lot behind the statue and tried to find their cars in the darkness that grew thicker as they stepped away from Harvey's glow.

"Over here!" I heard them shout. "I know the car's right over here!"

I walked to the lot, carried along by the crowd. But soon I found myself moving beyond the asphalt toward the same grass that had made my ankles damp nearly fifty years before when my father and I had crossed this lawn on Sunday visits to Harvey's throne.

I kept my footing. It was as if I remembered every cut and every rise on the hill where Harvey sat. Without thinking, I stepped across a rivulet that I remembered from my childhood (though I couldn't see it late at night), walked down Sage, and turned the corner to my house. I headed up Crescent, the way I would have on my bike, and knew exactly when to bend toward Evergreen.

My mother also knew the bends, even when Alzheimer's cut memory from her brain.

The police had often found Annabelle wandering the neighborhood, and brought her home. But she was never really lost. She never left the Park.

My father sometimes would fall asleep on the sofa, exhausted by the constant care Annabelle Coyne required. In the moment when he drifted off, my mother would be out the door and down the street.

A familiar patrol car would soon be seen in the Park, summoned by my father when he woke. The car would follow the same roads it always did when Tom Coyne called—first drive the four straight borders of the original neighborhood (Archwood Avenue, Brown Street, Wilbeth Road, and South Main) and then slowly wind its way down side streets to the interior of our neighborhood.

Sometimes the car would stop by the shelter house positioned at the east edge of the park, near the elementary school. An officer would shout my mother's name through a speaker, startling children on swings and causing teens hitting tennis balls to snap their heads toward the sound and ruin their serves.

Patrolmen often found my mother there. Or sometimes on Aster Avenue in front of the Lucky Store that closed in 1982, staring in the window at shoes no one else could see.

Annabelle Coyne never crossed outside the boundaries of this place where she had lived so long. She could no longer read, so the names of streets on corner signs were not what saved her. There was no friend left to signal from a window along the way, and traffic lights may as well have not been swinging in the summer air, for all the good they did directing her.

What saved my mother was something invisible, yet so strong that it lasted longer than her brain. It was more than just the memory of Harvey's curvy streets. It was closer to sonar, a way of reading echoes underground.

As I crossed my street, I felt this power in myself for the first time.

I stood by the mailbox that had been on the corner of Crescent and Evergreen all my life, and still was there. Touching it to keep my balance, I turned to look at our house. I could see a small curtain in the attic window. The new owners had made a room where boxes and my father's silver saxophone once had sat.

There were no thick drapes with rubber backing moving on traverse rods in the living room, like the ones my mother pulled at night, but balloon valances in maroon and beige, and swags. Puckers of fabric, like rows of lips, floated everywhere on heavy wooden rods.

I could see lights in a window, so I stared through the glass and let my eyes focus.

I saw myself sitting on the floor of the living room looking through my dad's magnifying glass at words in his crossword puzzle dictionary. I would lift the lens as high as it would go, making the letters as big as they could get before they blurred. Then I would adjust the glass until the words were black and clear.

I saw my mother sitting in a small chair reading a James Hilton novel abridged in a Reader's Digest *condensed book. Sometimes she'd lean over and rub the corns on her small toes with the palms of her hands.*

And I saw Tom Coyne. He was lying on the sofa shaving his whiskers with his Norelco, looking first at me on the floor and then out the window. I swear he was looking right at the older me standing by the mailbox looking in at him.

He was nervous, so maybe when he stared outside what he really saw was a wrecking ball, not me.

Or maybe he did see me, and that's why he was terrified.

He may have wondered if I would ever have the courage to listen to a prophet, much less ever be one. Would I have the wisdom to not be fooled and the strength to let my heart burst from my body with love? Would I have the courage to live, and then to die?

The questions I felt in my father's eyes bored into me until they became my own.

Would I ever have my father's courage, which he wore with such lumbering grace? Would I ever learn what it meant to be the daughter of rubber?

The daughter of Thomas William Coyne?

≈≈≈

I had not come to the Rededication to represent my father, as I had thought. I had come to find him. I knew that now.

I had come to remember him, and his hard lessons. They were my true Firestone heritage.

They were everything I had, now that he was gone.

⋙⋘

I crossed the street again and turned down Crescent. No picture in my family album was as clear to me as the image I'd just seen through the window of my own house. I knew I'd remember it. I knew I'd remember everything. I would never forget my father. Even if memory one day failed me, I would hear Tom Coyne's words echo underground when I walked the streets he'd brought me to.

I would go to the statue one last time before I drove away. I would close my eyes, let the wind blow through my hair, picture my father lifting me up into Harvey's arms.

When I was young, I thought those bronze arms were the strongest thing in the whole world.

But I was wrong.

It was my father's heart.

SOURCES

⧫⧫⧫

Akron, Ohio, has been fortunate to have had more than its share of fine historians and historical agencies eager to preserve its history and rich detail. During my research, I consulted Arthur H. Blower's *Akron at the Turn of the Century, 1890–1913,* published in 1962 by the Summit County Historical Society; *A Centennial History of Akron, 1825–1925,* published in 1925 by the Summit County Historical Society; Harry Christiansen's *Northern Ohio's Interurbans and Rapid Transit Railways,* published in 1965 by Berea; William B. Doyle's *Centennial History of Summit County, Ohio and Representative Citizens,* published in 1908 by Biographical in Chicago; Karl H. Grismer's *Akron and Summit County,* published in 1952 by the Summit County Historical Society; Scott Dix Kenfield's three-volume *Akron and Summit County Ohio, 1825–1928,* published in 1928 by Clarke in Chicago; Samuel A. Lane's *Fifty Years and Over of Akron and Summit County* (the author identifies himself as "ex-sheriff"), published in 1892 by Beacon; John S. Murphy, Kathleen A. Kochanski, and Angela K. Schumacher's *Akron Family Album,* published in 2001 by the *Akron Beacon Journal;* Oscar Eugene Olin's *Akron and Environs,* published in 1917 by Lewis in Chicago; William Henry Perrin's *History of Summit County,* published in 1881 by Baskin in Chicago; and the index to *Fifty Years and Over of Akron and Summit County,* compiled by Craig Wilson (with the assistance of Betty Fleming) and published by the Akron Summit County Chapter of Ohio Genealogical Society in 1986.

I must devote a separate line to C. R. Quine's *The Old Wolf Ledge,* published in 1958 by the Summit County Historical Society. Because my memoir and the history of my own life are so intimately tied to the story of Goosetown, I am forever in this local historian's debt.

I would like to acknowledge a few contemporary historians of Akron history whose work has been especially important to my own. These influential books include George Knepper's *Akron: City at the Summit,* published in 1981 by Continental in Tulsa; Frances McGovern's *Written on the Hills: The Making of the Akron Landscape,* published in 1996 by University of Akron Press, as well as her *Fun, Cheap, & Easy: My Life in Ohio Politics, 1949–1964,* published in 2002 by University of Akron Press; Ken Nichols's *Yesterday's Akron,* published in 1975 by Seemann in Miami; Carolyn Vogenitz's *Portage Lakes Then & Now,* published in 1999 by Waterside; Abe Zaidan's *Akron: Rising Toward the Twenty-First Century,* published in 1990 by Windsor in Chatsworth, California.

Information about Firestone Park, as well as Akron architecture and other model company towns, was invaluable to me. The detail of my own memory was enhanced (and sometimes corrected) by works such as these: Lois E. Finley's *Mosaic of Memories: Fifty Years 1926–1976, Garfield High School, Akron, Ohio,* published about 1976; John S. Garner's *The Model Company Town: Urban Design through Private Enterprise in Nineteenth-Century New England,* published in 1984 by the University of Massachusetts Press; *Historic Conservation in Akron: A Plan for Managing Resources,* published in March of 1978 by the Department of Planning and Urban Development; Clarice Finley Lewis's *A History of Firestone Park,* printed by the Firestone Park Citizens Council in 1986 (I am forever grateful for the meticulous detail of this small but rich volume); Kevan Delany Frazier's master's thesis, *Model Industrial Subdivisions: Goodyear Heights and Firestone Park and the Town Planning Movement in Akron, Ohio, 1910–1920,* completed in 1994 for Kent State University; Jim Paulau and John Vittum's article, "Firestone Park," in the brochure, *PTP Tour of Houses, June 18, 1992,* p. [1–4]; Kris Runberg Smith's *Housing with Dignity: Fifty Years of the Akron Metropolitan Housing Authority,* published in 1991 by the Summit County Historical Society; Katherine Cole Stevenson and H. Ward Jandl's *Houses by Mail: A Guide to Houses from Sears, Roebuck and Company,* published in 1986 by Wiley in New York.

I am grateful to scholars who have helped preserve the history of rubber, many of them focusing on the role of Akron companies in all of this. No source was more significant in my understanding of Akron's rubber history than Steve Love and David Giffels's *Wheels of Fortune: The Story of Rubber in Akron,* published in 1991 by the University of Akron Press. I also consulted Hugh Allen's *Rubber's Home Town: The Real-Life Story of Akron,* published in 1949 by Stratford in New York; *Job Descriptions in the Rubber Industry, 1939–1946,* compiled by the Ohio State Employment Service; Bruce Meyer's *The Once and Future Union: The Rise and Fall of the United Rubber Workers, 1935–1995,* published in 2002 by the University of Akron Press; Daniel Nelson's *American Rubber Workers & Organized Labor 1900–1941,* published in 1988 by Princeton University Press; "Rubber Slavery at Akron," a story by "a rubber worker" that appeared in the *Industrial Pioneer* on Aug. 1925, p. 3–5, 45; Charles Slack's *Noble Obsession: Charles Goodyear, Thomas Hancock, and the Race to Unlock the Greatest Industrial Secret of the Nineteenth Century,* published in 2002 by Hyperion in New York; Donald N. Sull's "The Dynamics of Standing Still: Firestone Tire & Rubber and the Radial Revolution," published in *Business History Review* 73.3 (fall 1999), p. 430–64; Howard Wolf and Ralph Wolf's *Rubber: A Story of Glory and Greed,* published in 1936 by Covici in New York.

This is a memoir, not a local history, so many of the stories about Harvey Firestone and the Firestone Tire & Rubber Company come out of my family's telling—or living—of them. But supplemental detail was added at times from *Non-Skids* and *Beacon Journals,* as well as Paul Dickson and William D. Hickman's *Firestone: A Legend. A Century. A Celebration,* edited by Nelson Eddy and published in 2000 by Bridgestone/Firestone for the Firestone Centennial; Harvey S. Firestone Sr.'s *Men and Rubber: The Story of Business,* written with Samuel Crowther in 1926 for Doubleday in New York; Harvey S. Firestone Jr.'s *The Romance and Drama of the Rubber Industry,* published in 1933 by Firestone; Alfred Lief's two books published in 1951 by McGraw in New York—*The Firestone Story* and *Harvey Firestone: Free Man of Enterprise;* Adrian Paradis's *Harvey S. Firestone: Young Rubber Pioneer,* published in 1968 by Bobbs-Merrill; *Pioneer and Pacemaker,* an undated publication about the founder published by Firestone.

Detail about the processing of rubber came mainly from my conversations with chemist Ben Kastein, but I also referred to *Evaluating Carbon Black for the Rubber Industry in the Huber Laboratory,* published in 1936 by Huber in New York; Vladimir M. Makarov and Valerij F. Drozdovski's *Reprocessing of Tyres and Rubber Wastes: Recycling from the Rubber Products Industry,* translated by Vladimir B. Sokolov and published in 1991 by Ellis in West Sussex; Maurice Morton's *Introduction to Rubber Technology,* published in 1959 by Reinhold in New York; Henry C. Pearson's *Rubber Machinery,* published in 1920 by India in New York; George G. Winspear's *The Vanderbilt Rubber Handbook,* published in 1968 by Vanderbilt in New York. Essential information about mining, as well as Akron's particular mining history, came from the *Division of Mines Report,* published in 1965 and 1968 by the State of Ohio; Donald Fred Schaefer's *A Quantitative Description and Analysis of the Growth of the Pennsylvania Anthracite Coal Industry 1820 to 1865,* published in 1977 by Arno in New York; Sherry L. Weisgarber's *1990 Report on Ohio Mineral Industries,* a report compiled in 1991 for the State of Ohio. Frances McGovern's book *Written on the Hills* also contains an eloquent and accurate history of Akron's bedrock that I found extremely useful.

Background about the history of blacks and Appalachians in Akron, Ohio (including their migrations to Rubber Town), came from Shirla Robinson McClain's *The Contributions of Blacks in Akron: 1825–1975,* edited by the Akron Gallery of Black History Curriculum Committee for the University of Akron in 1996; A. Kingsberry's *Akron Negro Directory,* compiled in March of 1940; *A Report on Appalachians in Akron, Ohio,* prepared in 1978 by the Ohio Urban Appalachian Awareness Project in Cincinnati, Ohio.

In addition to interviewing my cousin Carol about her personal experience with polio, I read background about poliomyelitis in Tony Gould's *A Summer Plague: Polio and Its Survivors,* published in 1995 by Yale University Press; John R. Paul's *A History of Poliomyelitis,* published in 1971 by Yale University Press; Jane S. Smith's *Patenting the Sun: Polio and the Salk Vaccine,* published in 1990 by Morrow in New York; "What Schools Can Do to Help Control Poliomyelitis," a publication by the Poliomyelitis Advisory Committee in 1951.

A variety of maps let me see Akron and Firestone in ways I never had before. Among other resources, I consulted *Akron Historic Landmark Survey,* completed in 1980 by the City of Akron, Department of Planning and Urban Development; the *Atlas and Industrial Geography of Summit County, Ohio, Compiled from County Records and Actual Survey,* published in 1910 by Rectigraph; *Illustrated Summit County, Ohio,* published in 1891 by the Akron Map and Atlas Co., and reprinted in 1992 by Bookmark in Knightstown, Indiana; Sanborn maps of Akron, Ohio, prepared by Sanborn in Chicago in 1968 and 1969, vols. 1 and 5; Bruce M. Stave's edited collection, *Fire Insurance Maps from the Sanborn Map Company Archives, Late 19th Century to 1990, Ohio,* published in 1992 by University Publications in Bethesda. I also relied heavily on plat maps of Firestone Park found in the Akron Courthouse and the University of Akron archives.